Financial Institutions and Services Series

AF753250

HEDGE FUNDS: REGULATION AND NONREGULATION

FINANCIAL INSTITUTIONS AND SERVICES SERIES

Stock Exchanges, IPO's and Mutual funds
E. Klein (Editor)
2004 ISBN: 1-59454-173-6

Global Banking Issues
E. Klein (Editor)
2005 ISBN: 1-59454-172-8

Financial Institutions and Development
E. Klein (Editor)
2005 ISBN: 1-59454-177-9

Capital Formation, Governance and Banking
E. Klein (Editor)
2005 ISBN: 1-59454-191-4

U. S. Coins: The Price of a Penny
Walter M. Carvalho (Editor)
2009 ISBN: : 978-1-60692-939-1

Hedge Funds: Regulation and Nonregulation
Yeram E. Torrey (Editor)
2009. ISBN: 978-1-60692-041-1

Financial Institutions and Services Series

HEDGE FUNDS: REGULATION AND NONREGULATION

YERAM E. TORREY
EDITOR

Nova Science Publishers, Inc.
New York

Copyright © 2009 by Nova Science Publishers, Inc.

All rights reserved. No part of this book may be reproduced, stored in a retrieval system or transmitted in any form or by any means: electronic, electrostatic, magnetic, tape, mechanical photocopying, recording or otherwise without the written permission of the Publisher.

For permission to use material from this book please contact us:
Telephone 631-231-7269; Fax 631-231-8175
Web Site: http://www.novapublishers.com

NOTICE TO THE READER

The Publisher has taken reasonable care in the preparation of this book, but makes no expressed or implied warranty of any kind and assumes no responsibility for any errors or omissions. No liability is assumed for incidental or consequential damages in connection with or arising out of information contained in this book. The Publisher shall not be liable for any special, consequential, or exemplary damages resulting, in whole or in part, from the readers' use of, or reliance upon, this material.

Independent verification should be sought for any data, advice or recommendations contained in this book. In addition, no responsibility is assumed by the publisher for any injury and/or damage to persons or property arising from any methods, products, instructions, ideas or otherwise contained in this publication.

This publication is designed to provide accurate and authoritative information with regard to the subject matter covered herein. It is sold with the clear understanding that the Publisher is not engaged in rendering legal or any other professional services. If legal or any other expert assistance is required, the services of a competent person should be sought. FROM A DECLARATION OF PARTICIPANTS JOINTLY ADOPTED BY A COMMITTEE OF THE AMERICAN BAR ASSOCIATION AND A COMMITTEE OF PUBLISHERS.

LIBRARY OF CONGRESS CATALOGING-IN-PUBLICATION DATA
Available upon request
ISBN: 978-1-60692-041-1

Published by Nova Science Publishers, Inc. ✣ New York

CONTENTS

PREFACE

Since the 1998 near collapse of Long-Term Capital Management (LTCM), a large hedge fund—a pooled investment vehicle that is privately managed and often engages in active trading of various types of securities and commodity futures and options—the number of hedge funds has grown, and they have attracted investments from institutional investors such as pension plans. Hedge funds generally are recognized as important sources of liquidity and as holders and managers of risks in the capital markets. Although the market impacts of recent hedge fund near collapses were less severe than that of LTCM, they recalled concerns about risks associated with hedge funds and they highlighted the continuing relevance of questions raised over LTCM. This book (1) describes how federal financial regulators oversee hedge fund-related activities under their existing authorities; (2) examines what measures investors, creditors, and counterparties have taken to impose market discipline on hedge funds; and (3) explores the potential for systemic risk from hedge fund-related activities and describes actions regulators have taken to address this risk.

In: Hedge Funds: Regulation and Nonregulation ISBN: 978-1-60692-041-1
Editor: Yeram E. Torrey, pp. 1-6 © 2009 Nova Science Publishers, Inc.

WHAT GAO FOUND*

Under the existing regulatory structure, the Securities and Exchange Commission and Commodity Futures Trading Commission can provide direct oversight of registered hedge fund advisers, and along with federal bank regulators, they monitor hedge fund-related activities conducted at their regulated entities. Since LTCM's near collapse, regulators generally have increased reviews—by such means as targeted examinations—of systems and policies of their regulated entities to mitigate counterparty credit risks, including those involving hedge funds. Although some examinations found that banks generally have strengthened practices for managing risk exposures to hedge funds, regulators recommended that they enhance firmwide risk management systems and practices, including expanded stress testing. Regulated entities have the responsibility to practice prudent risk management standards, but prudent standards do not guarantee prudent practices. As such, it will be important for regulators to show continued vigilance in overseeing hedge fund-related activities.

According to market participants, hedge fund advisers have improved disclosures and transparency about their operations since LTCM as a result of industry guidance issued and pressure from investors and creditors and counterparties (such as prime brokers). But market participants also suggested that not all investors have the capacity to analyze the information they receive from hedge funds. Regulators and market participants said that creditors and counterparties have generally conducted more due diligence and tightened their credit standards for hedge funds. However, several factors may limit the effectiveness of market discipline or illustrate failures to properly exercise it. For example, because most large hedge funds use multiple prime brokers as service

* Excerpted from GAO Report GAO-08-200, dated January 2008.

providers, no one broker may have all the data necessary to assess the total leverage of a hedge fund client. Further, if the risk controls of creditors and counterparties are inadequate, their actions may not prevent hedge funds from taking excessive risk. These factors can contribute to conditions that create systemic risk if breakdowns in market discipline and risk controls are sufficiently severe that losses by hedge funds in turn cause significant losses at key intermediaries or in financial markets.

Financial regulators and industry participants remain concerned about the adequacy of counterparty credit risk management at major financial institutions because it is a key factor in controlling the potential for hedge funds to become a source of systemic risk. Regulators have used risk-focused and principles-based approaches to better understand the potential for systemic risk and respond more effectively to financial shocks that threaten to affect the financial system. For instance, regulators have collaborated to examine some hedge fund activities across regulated entities. The President's Working Group has taken steps such as issuing guidance and forming two private sector groups to develop best practices to enhance market discipline. GAO views these as positive steps, but it is too soon to evaluate their effectiveness.

Why GAO Did this Study

Since the 1998 near collapse of Long-Term Capital Management (LTCM), a large hedge fund—a pooled investment vehicle that is privately managed and often engages in active trading of various types of securities and commodity futures and options—the number of hedge funds has grown, and they have attracted investments from institutional investors such as pension plans. Hedge funds generally are recognized as important sources of liquidity and as holders and managers of risks in the capital markets. Although the market impacts of recent hedge fund near collapses were less severe than that of LTCM, they recalled concerns about risks associated with hedge funds and they highlighted the continuing relevance of questions raised over LTCM. This report (1) describes how federal financial regulators oversee hedge fund-related activities under their existing authorities; (2) examines what measures investors, creditors, and counterparties have taken to impose market discipline on hedge funds; and (3) explores the potential for systemic risk from hedge fund-related activities and describes actions regulators have taken to address this risk. In conducting this study, GAO reviewed regulators' policy documents and examinations and industry reports and interviewed regulatory and industry officials, and academics.

Regulators only provided technical comments on a draft of this report, which GAO has incorporated into the report as appropriate.

ABBREVIATIONS

CDO	collateralized debt obligation
CEA	Commodity Exchange Act of 1936
CFTC	Commodity Futures Trading Commission
CPO	commodity pool operator
CTA	commodity trading advisor
CRMPG	Counterparty Risk Management Policy Group
CSE	Consolidated Supervised Entity
DB	defined benefit
DOL	Department of Labor
ERISA	Employee Retirement Income Security Act of 1974
FCM	futures commission merchant
FDIC	Federal Deposit Insurance Corporation
FRBNY	Federal Reserve Bank of New York
FSA	Financial Services Authority (United Kingdom)
IOSCO	International Organization of Securities Commissions
LTCM	Long-Term Capital Management
LTRS	large trader reporting system
MFA	Managed Funds Association
NFA	National Futures Association
OCC	Office of the Comptroller of the Currency
OTC	over-the-counter
OTS	Office of Thrift Supervision
PPA	Pension Protection Act of 2006
PPM	private placement memorandum
PWG	President's Working Group on Financial Markets
RADAR	Risk Assessment Database for Analysis and Reporting
SEC	Securities and Exchange Commission

January 24, 2008

The Honorable Barney Frank
Chairman

Committee on Financial Services House of Representatives

The Honorable Paul E. Kanjorski
Chairman
Subcommittee on Capital Markets, Insurance and
Government Sponsored Enterprises House of Representatives

The Honorable Michael E. Capuano
House of Representatives

In recent years, hedge funds have grown rapidly.[1] According to industry estimates, from 1998 to early 2007, the number of funds grew from more than 3,000 to more than 9,000, and assets under management from more than $200 billion to more than $2 trillion globally.[2] An estimated $1.5 trillion of these assets is managed by U.S. hedge fund advisers. Hedge funds are key players in many financial markets. For example, hedge funds reportedly account for more than 40 percent of the trading volume in the U.S. leveraged loan market, more than 85 percent of the distressed debt market, and more than 80 percent of certain credit derivatives markets.[3] Institutional investors, such as endowments, foundations, insurance companies, and pension plans, seeking to diversify their risks and increase returns, have invested in hedge funds and contributed to the rapid growth in these funds.

As active market participants, hedge funds generally are recognized to provide benefits to financial markets by enhancing liquidity and promoting market efficiency and price discovery.[4] Especially in volatile markets, hedge funds are generally willing to assume risks that more regulated financial institutions are unwilling or unable to assume. Additionally, they are recognized to spur financial innovation and help to reallocate financial risk. Nevertheless, the rapid growth of funds that may adopt similar investment strategies in interconnected markets with rapid trading strategies raises questions as to whether large losses from one or more hedge funds could cause widespread difficulties at other firms, in other market segments, or in the financial system as a whole. For example, hedge funds may impose losses on their creditors and counterparties and thereby disrupt the credit availability to financial markets or through market disruptions that could accompany liquidation of funds' positions.[5]

Market discipline plays a primary role, supplemented by indirect regulatory oversight of commercial banks and securities and futures firms, in constraining risk taking and leveraging by hedge fund managers (advisers). Market participants (e.g., investors, creditors, and counterparties) impose market discipline by rewarding well-managed hedge funds and reducing their exposure to risky, poorly managed hedge funds. However, according to several sources, for market discipline to be effective, (1) investors, creditors, and counterparties must have access to, and act upon, sufficient and timely information to assess a fund's risk profile; (2) investors, creditors, and counterparties must have sound risk management policies, procedures, and systems to evaluate and limit their credit risk exposures to hedge funds; and (3) creditors and counterparties must increase the costs or decrease the availability of credit to their hedge fund clients as the creditworthiness of the latter changes.

Inadequate market discipline is often cited as a contributing factor to the near collapse in 1998 of Long-Term Capital Management (LTCM), a large highly leveraged hedge fund. The subsequent 1999 report by the President's Working Group on Financial Markets (PWG) questioned the adequacy of (1) market discipline that some creditors and counterparties (commercial and investment banks, including their prime brokerage business and futures firms) imposed on LTCM's risk-taking activities, and (2) LTCM's disclosure and risk management practices.[6] The report also raised questions about the risk management practices of these entities and the ability of federal financial regulators to supervise effectively the large creditors and counterparties that extended credit to hedge funds. In its 1999 report, the PWG made recommendations to enhance market discipline and the risk management practices of market participants.[7] Since LTCM, other hedge funds have experienced near collapses or failures.[8] Despite a few notable failures, hedge funds overall seem to have held up well, and their counterparties have not sustained material losses in the market turmoil that began in the summer of 2007.[9] Although the market impacts of the recent cases were less severe than that of LTCM, they recalled concerns about risks associated with hedge funds and they highlighted the continuing relevance of questions raised over LTCM.

Given the growing importance and continuing evolution of the hedge fund sector since LTCM, you asked us to study the risks hedge funds may pose to the financial markets and how hedge fund creditors and counterparties and the regulatory framework can address those risks. Accordingly, this report (1) describes how federal financial regulators provide oversight of hedge fund-related activities under their existing authorities; (2) examines what measures investors, creditors, and counterparties have taken to impose market discipline on hedge funds; and (3) explores the potential for systemic risk from hedge fund-related activities and actions regulators have taken to address this risk.[10] In addition, we provide information on pension plan investments in hedge funds in appendix II.

In conducting our work, we reviewed and analyzed relevant regulatory examination documentation and enforcement cases from federal financial regulators. This included examination documentation and enforcement cases from the following federal banking regulators—Office of the Comptroller of the Currency (OCC), Board of Governors of the Federal Reserve System (Federal Reserve), Federal Reserve Bank of New York (FRBNY), and Federal Deposit Insurance Corporation (FDIC); a federal securities regulator—Securities and Exchange Commission (SEC); and futures markets regulators—Commodity Futures Trading Commission (CFTC) and National Futures Association (NFA).[11] We also analyzed relevant laws and regulations, speeches, testimonies, studies, and prior GAO reports, as well as principles and guidelines that the PWG issued about private pools of capital—including hedge funds, PWG protocols, and relevant industry best practices for hedge fund advisers, creditors, and counterparties. We interviewed officials representing the U.S. regulators identified above and the Office of Thrift Supervision (OTS), the PWG, Department of Labor (DOL), and the Department of the Treasury (Treasury).[12] We also interviewed officials of the United Kingdom's Financial Services Authority (FSA), as well as representatives from market participants such as commercial and investment banks, large hedge funds, pension industry participants, credit rating agencies, a risk management firm, a hedge fund law firm, trade groups representing hedge funds and institutional investors, and academics. We conducted this performance audit from September 2006 to January 2008 in accordance with generally accepted government auditing standards. Those standards require that we plan and perform the audit to obtain sufficient, appropriate evidence to provide a reasonable basis for our findings and conclusions based on our audit objectives. We believe that the evidence obtained provides a reasonable basis for our findings and conclusions based on our audit objectives. Appendix I provides a detailed description of our scope and methodology.

In: Hedge Funds: Regulation and Nonregulation ISBN: 978-1-60692-041-1
Editor: Yeram E. Torrey, pp. 7-10 © 2009 Nova Science Publishers, Inc.

Chapter 1

RESULTS IN BRIEF

Under the existing regulatory structure, SEC and CFTC regulate those hedge fund advisers that are registered with them, but SEC, CFTC, as well as the federal bank regulators (collectively, financial regulators) monitor hedge fund-related activities of other regulated entities such as broker- dealers and commercial banks.[13] Specifically, SEC regulates an estimated 1,991 hedge fund advisers that are registered as investment advisers, which include 49 of the largest U.S. hedge fund advisers that account for about one-third of hedge funds' assets under management in the United States.[14] As registered investment advisers, hedge fund advisers are subject to SEC examinations and reporting, record keeping, and disclosure requirements. In fiscal year 2006, SEC examined 321 hedge fund advisers and identified issues (such as information disclosure, reporting and filing, personal trading, and asset valuation) that are not exclusive to hedge funds. Also, in 2004 SEC established a program to oversee the large internationally active securities firms on a consolidated basis. These securities firms have significant interaction with hedge funds through affiliates previously not overseen by SEC. One aspect of this program is to examine how the securities firms manage various risk exposures, including those from hedge fund-related activities such as providing prime brokerage services and acting as creditors and counterparties. Similarly, CFTC regulates those hedge fund advisers registered as commodity pool operators (CPO) or commodity trading advisors (CTA).[15] CFTC has authorized NFA to conduct day-to-day monitoring of registered CPOs and CTAs; in fiscal year 2006, NFA examinations of CPOs included six of the largest U.S. hedge fund advisers. In addition, SEC, CFTC, and bank regulators can use their existing authorities—to establish capital standards and reporting requirements, conduct risk-based examinations, and take enforcement actions—to oversee activities, including those involving hedge funds, of broker-dealers, of futures commission merchants, and of banks, respectively. While none of the regulators we interviewed specifically monitored hedge fund activities on an ongoing basis, generally regulators have increased reviews—by such means as targeted examinations—of systems and policies to mitigate counterparty credit risk at the large regulated entities. For instance, from 2004 to 2007, FRBNY conducted various reviews—including horizontal reviews—of credit risk management practices that involved hedge fund-related activities at several large banks.[16] On the basis of the results, FRBNY noted that the banks generally had strengthened practices for managing risk exposures to hedge funds, but the banks could further enhance firmwide risk management systems and practices, including expanded stress testing.[17] Regulated entities have the responsibility to practice prudent risk management standards, but prudent standards do not guarantee prudent practices. As such, it will be important for regulators to show continued vigilance in overseeing the hedge fund-related activities of regulated institutions.

Since the near collapse of LTCM in 1998, investors, creditors, and counterparties have increased their efforts to impose market discipline on hedge funds. However, regulators and market participants also identified issues that limit the effectiveness of these efforts. Investors, creditors, and counterparties impose market discipline on hedge funds by providing more funding or better terms to those hedge funds willing to disclose credible information about the fund's risks and prospective returns. According to market participants doing business with larger hedge funds, hedge fund advisers have improved disclosure and become more transparent about their operations, including risk management practices, partly as a result of recent increases in investments by institutional investors with fiduciary responsibilities, such as pension plans, and guidance provided by regulators and industry groups. Despite the requirement that fund investors be sophisticated, some market participants suggested that not all prospective investors have the capacity or retain the expertise to analyze the information they receive from hedge funds, and some may choose to invest in a hedge fund largely as a result of its prior returns and may fail to fully evaluate its risks. Regulators and market participants also said creditors and counterparties have been conducting more extensive due diligence and monitoring risk exposures to their hedge fund clients since LTCM. The creditors and counterparties we interviewed said that they have exercised market discipline by tightening their credit standards for hedge funds and demanding greater disclosure. However, several factors limit the effectiveness of market discipline or illustrate failures to properly exercise it. For example, most large hedge funds use multiple prime brokers as service providers. Thus, no one broker may have all the data necessary to assess the total leverage used by a hedge fund client. Further, the actions of creditors and counterparties may not fully prevent hedge funds from taking excessive risk if these creditors' and counterparties' risk controls are inadequate. For example, the risk controls may not keep pace with the increasing complexity of financial instruments and investment strategies that hedge funds employ. Similarly, regulators have been concerned that in competing for hedge fund clients, creditors sometimes relaxed credit standards. These factors can contribute to conditions that create the potential for systemic risk if breakdowns in market discipline and the risk controls of creditors and counterparties are sufficiently severe that losses by hedge funds in turn cause significant losses at key intermediaries or in financial markets.

Although financial regulators and market participants recognize that the enhanced efforts by investors, creditors, and counterparties since LTCM impose greater market discipline on hedge funds, some remain concerned that hedge funds' activities are a potential source of systemic risk. Counterparty credit risk arises when hedge funds enter into transactions, including derivatives contracts, with regulated financial institutions.[18] Some regulators regard counterparty credit risk as the primary channel for potentially creating systemic risk. As discussed earlier, some regulators questioned whether some creditors and counterparties could manage counterparty credit risk effectively. In addition to counterparty credit risk, other factors such as trading behavior can create conditions that contribute to systemic risk. Given certain market conditions, the simultaneous liquidation of similar positions by hedge funds that hold large positions on the same side of a trade could lead to losses or a liquidity crisis that might aggravate financial distress. Recognizing that market discipline cannot eliminate the potential systemic risk posed by hedge funds and others, regulators have been taking steps to better understand the potential for systemic risk and respond more effectively to financial disruptions that can spread across markets. For instance, they have examined particular hedge fund activities across regulated entities, mainly through international multilateral efforts. The PWG has issued guidelines that provide a framework for addressing risks associated with hedge funds and implemented protocols to respond to market turmoil. Finally, the PWG recently established two private sector committees comprising hedge fund advisers and investors to address investor protection and systemic risk concerns, including counterparty credit risk management issues. We view these actions as positive steps to address systemic risk, but it is too soon to evaluate their effectiveness.

We provided a draft of this report to CFTC, DOL, Federal Reserve, FDIC, OCC, OTS, SEC, and Treasury for their review and comment. None of the agencies provided written comments. All except for FDIC and OTS provided technical comments, which we have incorporated into the report as appropriate.

In: Hedge Funds: Regulation and Nonregulation ISBN: 978-1-60692-041-1
Editor: Yeram E. Torrey, pp. 11-12 © 2009 Nova Science Publishers, Inc.

Chapter 2

BACKGROUND

Hedge funds typically are organized as limited partnerships or limited liability companies, and are structured and operated in a manner that enables the fund and its advisers to qualify for exemptions from certain federal securities laws and regulations that apply to other investment pools, such as mutual funds.[19] In addition, hedge funds operate to qualify for exemptions from certain registration and disclosure requirements of federal securities laws (including the Securities Act of 1933 and the Securities Exchange Act of 1934). For example, hedge funds must refrain from advertising to the general public and can solicit participation in the fund from only certain large institutions and wealthy individuals.[20] Although certain advisers may be exempt from registration requirements, they remain subject to anti-fraud (including insider trading), anti- manipulation, and large trading position reporting rules. For example, upon acquiring a significant ownership position in a particular publicly traded security or holding a certain level of futures or options positions, a hedge fund adviser may be required to file a report disclosing the adviser's or hedge fund's holdings with SEC or positions with CFTC, as applicable.

Hedge funds have significant business relationships with the largest regulated commercial and investment banks. Hedge funds act as trading counterparties for a wide range of over-the-counter (OTC) derivatives and other financing transactions. They also act as clients through their purchase of clearing and other services and as borrowers through their use of margin loans from prime brokers.

Hedge funds generally are not restricted by regulation in their choice of investment strategies, as are mutual funds. They may invest in a wide variety of financial instruments, including stocks and bonds, currencies, OTC derivatives, futures contracts, and other assets. Most hedge fund trading strategies are dynamic, often changing rapidly to adjust to fluid market conditions. To seek to generate "absolute returns" (performance that exceeds and has low correlation with stock and bond markets returns), advisers may use leverage, short selling, and a variety of sophisticated investment strategies and techniques.[21] However, while hedge funds frequently borrow or trade in products with leverage to magnify their returns, leverage also can increase their losses. Appendix III provides examples of investment strategies used by hedge funds.

Advisers of hedge funds commonly receive a fixed compensation of 2 percent of assets under management plus 20 percent of the fund's annual profits. Some fund advisers can command higher fees. Since this compensation scheme rewards hedge fund advisers for exceptional performance, but does not directly penalize them for inferior performance, advisers could be tempted to pursue excessively risky investment strategies that might produce exceptional returns. To discourage excessive risk taking, investors generally insist that the advisers and principals also personally invest in their funds to more closely align principals' interests with those of fund investors.

In: Hedge Funds: Regulation and Nonregulation ISBN: 978-1-60692-041-1
Editor: Yeram E. Torrey, pp. 13-26 © 2009 Nova Science Publishers, Inc.

Chapter 3

HEDGE FUNDS GENERALLY ARE SUBJECT TO LIMITED DIRECT OVERSIGHT, BUT REGULATORY FOCUS HAS INCREASED SINCE LTCM

SEC's ability to directly oversee hedge fund advisers is limited to those that are required to register or voluntarily register with SEC as investment advisers. Recent examinations of registered advisers raised concerns in areas such as disclosure, reporting and filing, personal trading, and asset valuation. Also, under a program established in 2004, SEC oversees, on a consolidated basis, some of the largest internationally active securities firms that engage in significant hedge fund-related activities. CFTC directly oversees registered CPOs and CTAs (some of which may be hedge fund advisers) through market surveillance, regulatory compliance surveillance, an examination program delegated to NFA, and enforcement actions. The banking regulators also monitor hedge fund-related activities at the institutions under their jurisdiction. For instance, in recent years regulators conducted targeted examinations and horizontal reviews that have focused on areas such as stress testing, leverage, liquidity, due diligence, and margining practices as well as overall credit risk management.

With Limited Authority to Regulate Hedge Funds, SEC Largely Monitors Hedge Fund Activities and Related Risks through Consolidated Supervision of Large Securities Firms

Registered hedge fund advisers are subject to the same disclosure requirements as all other registered investment advisers. These advisers must provide current information to both SEC and investors about their business practices and disciplinary history. Advisers also must maintain required books and records, and are subject to periodic examinations by SEC staff. Meanwhile, hedge funds, like other investors in publicly traded securities, are subject to various regulatory reporting requirements. For example, upon acquiring a 5 percent beneficial ownership position of a particular publicly traded security, a hedge fund may be required to file a report disclosing its holdings with SEC.[22] Also, any institutional investment adviser with investment discretion over accounts holding certain publicly traded equity securities valued at $100 million or more must file on a quarterly a report with SEC.[23] SEC also plans to propose new rule making that would require a registered adviser sponsoring a hedge fund to identify and provide some basic information to SEC about the hedge fund's gatekeepers, i.e., auditor, prime broker, custodian, and administrator.

In December 2004, SEC adopted an amendment to Rule 203(b)(3)-1, which had the effect of requiring certain hedge fund advisers that previously enjoyed the private adviser exemption from registration to register with SEC as investment advisers.[24] In June 2006, a federal court vacated the 2004 amendment to Rule 203(b)(3)-1.[25] According to SEC, when the rule was in effect (from February 1, 2006, through August 21, 2006), SEC was better able to identify hedge fund advisers. In August 2006, SEC estimated that 2,534 advisers that sponsored at least one hedge fund were registered with the agency. Since August 2006, SEC's ability to identify an adviser that manages a hedge fund has been further limited due to changes in filing requirements and to advisers that chose to retain registered status. As of April 2007, 488, or about 19 percent of the 2,534 advisers, had withdrawn their registrations. At the same time, 76 new registrants were added and some others changed their filing status, leaving an estimated 1,991 hedge fund advisers registered. While the list of registered hedge fund advisers is not all-inclusive, many of the largest hedge fund advisers—including 49 of the largest 78 U.S. hedge fund advisers—are registered. These 49 hedge fund advisers account for approximately $492 billion of assets under management, or about 33 percent of the estimated $1.5 trillion in hedge fund assets under management in the United States.[26]

SEC Examinations of Hedge Fund Advisers Identified Areas of Concern

In fiscal year 2006, SEC took additional steps to oversee hedge fund advisers by creating an examination module specifically for hedge fund advisers and providing training for examiners in hedge fund-related topics. The new examination module outlines how the examination of a hedge fund adviser generally begins with an analysis of the adviser's compliance program and the work of its chief compliance officer and uses a control scorecard as a guide. As part of this review of compliance programs, examiners inspect the typical activities of advisers and are expected to obtain a clear understanding of all activities of affiliates and how these activities may affect or conflict with those of the hedge fund adviser being examined. Examiners are to focus primarily on the following activities during their examinations of hedge fund advisers:

- portfolio management;
- brokerage arrangements and trading;
- personal trading by access persons;
- valuation of positions and calculations of net asset value;
- leverage;
- safety of clients' and funds' assets;
- performance calculations;
- fund investors and capital introduction;
- violations of domestic or foreign laws that may directly harm fund investors or other market participants, or cause harm to prime brokers;
- books and records, fund financial statements, and investor reporting;
- chief compliance officer, compliance culture, and program; and
- boards of directors for offshore funds (fiduciary duties to shareholders of the hedge funds and consistent disclosure to its investors).

In preparation for the registration of hedge fund advisers and because SEC does not have a dedicated group of examiners that focus on hedge funds, SEC and hedge fund industry officials noted the need for more experience and ongoing training of examiners on hedge funds' investment strategies and complex financial instruments. SEC developed a specialized training program to better familiarize its examiners with the operation of hedge funds to improve effectiveness of examinations of hedge fund advisers. In that regard, from October 2005 through October 2006, SEC held about 20 examiner training sessions on hedge fund-related topics. Industry participants were instructors in many of these sessions. These sessions covered topics such as hedge fund structure, hedge fund investment vehicles, identification and examination of conflicts of interests at hedge fund advisers, risk management, prime brokerage, valuation, current and future regulation, examination issues, and investment risk. SEC continues to offer hedge fund training to examiners and other staff on an ongoing voluntary basis.

SEC uses a risk-based examination approach to select investment advisers for inspections. Under this approach, higher-risk investment advisers are examined every 3 years.[27] One of the variables in determining risk level is the amount of assets under management. SEC officials told us that most hedge funds, even the larger ones, do not meet the dollar threshold to be automatically considered higher-risk. As part of the overall risk-based approach for conducting oversight of investment advisers, SEC uses a database application called Risk Assessment Database for Analysis and Reporting (RADAR), to identify the highest-risk areas designated by examiners and to develop and recommend regulatory responses to address these higher-risk areas. In fiscal year 2006, RADAR identified a number of hedge fund-related risk areas, which although not exclusive to hedge funds require additional regulatory attention, including the following:

- soft dollars (e.g., paying for a hedge fund's office space without disclosing it);
- market manipulation (e.g., the dissemination of false information to inflate the price of a stock);
- hedge fund custody and misappropriation (e.g., theft of hedge fund assets by its advisers);
- complexity of hedge fund products and suitability (e.g., inadequacy of policies and procedures to assess the complexity of financial instruments and the suitability of products for investors);
- prime brokerage relationships (e.g., potential conflicts of interest where prime brokers give hedge fund clients—who often pay large dollar amounts of commissions—priority over non-hedge fund clients regarding access to information/research);
- performance fees (e.g., incorrect calculation of performance fees);
- hedge fund valuation (e.g., inadequate policies and procedures to ensure that asset valuations are accurate);

- fund of funds' conflicts of interest (e.g., conflicts of interest between fund of funds advisers and their recommendation to a fund of hedge fund to invest in certain hedge funds);
- insider trading (e.g., trading on nonpublic information); and
- hedge fund suitability (e.g., inadequate policies and procedures to ensure the financial qualification of investors).

According to SEC officials, they plan to address these risks by primarily focusing on these areas during subsequent examinations.

As part of its fiscal year 2006 routine inspection program, SEC conducted examinations of 1,346 registered investment advisers, of which 321 were believed to have involved hedge fund advisers. SEC used its new hedge fund module, along with other modules as appropriate, to conduct the 321 examinations, which included 5 of the largest 78 U.S. hedge funds.[28] According to SEC officials, the 321 hedge fund advisers' examinations found that these advisers had the greatest deficiencies in the following areas: (1) information disclosures, reporting, and filing—e.g., private placement memorandum was outdated; (2) personal trading—e.g., quarterly reports were not filed or filed late for personal trading accounts; and (3) compliance rule—e.g., policies and procedures were inadequate to address compliance risks. Examiners also cited concerns with performance advertising and marketing of portfolio management, brokerage arrangement and execution, information processing and protection, safety of clients' funds and assets, pricing of clients' portfolios, trade allocations, and anti-money laundering.

In our review of 9 of the 321 examinations of hedge fund advisers, we found that examiners cited deficiencies in 8 of these examinations. Deficiencies found included all of the above mentioned categories except for trade allocations. For example, examiners identified concerns in 5 of the examinations regarding disclosures and in one of the examinations, for instance, the hedge fund adviser's marketing package did not disclose any material conditions, objectives, or investment strategies used to obtain the performance result portrayed. In another examination, the hedge fund adviser failed to adequately disclose to investors that a conflict of interest may be present when the hedge fund adviser places transactions through broker-dealers who have invested in the hedge fund.

According to SEC officials, 294 (or approximately 92 percent) of the 321 hedge fund advisers examined received deficiency letters.[29] Some 292 of them provided satisfactory responses to SEC that they had taken or would take appropriate corrective actions. Such actions can include advisers implementing policies and procedures to address deficiencies. Those hedge fund advisers that do not take or propose to take corrective actions for a material deficiency may be referred to SEC's Division of Enforcement (Enforcement) for enforcement actions. According to SEC, 23 of the 321 examinations resulted in enforcement referrals, and most of these referrals regarded situations in which the adviser appeared to have engaged in fraud that harmed its clients.

As part of its oversight activities, SEC has brought a number of enforcement actions involving hedge fund advisers. Sources of information that led to SEC enforcement cases included examinations, self-regulatory organizations, referrals, and tips. From October 1, 2001, to June 12, 2007, SEC brought a total of 3,937 enforcement cases, of which 113, or 2.9 percent, were hedge fund-related. These cases involve hedge fund advisers who misappropriated fund assets, engaged in insider trading, misrepresented portfolio performance, falsified their experience and credentials, or lied about past returns. As an example, in 2006, SEC brought a case against a hedge fund adviser and its former portfolio manager and charged them with making investment decisions based on nonpublic insider information that certain public offerings were about to be publicly announced. The hedge fund adviser agreed to pay approximately $5.7 million in disgorgement, prejudgment interest, and civil money penalty, and the former portfolio manager agreed to pay a civil money penalty of $110,000 and be barred from associating with an investment adviser for 3 years. SEC also has brought cases for inaccurate disclosure of trading strategies, undisclosed preferential treatment of hedge fund clients at the expense of other clients, market manipulation, insider trading, illegal short selling, and improper valuation of assets. During the same period, nine insider trading cases were brought against hedge fund advisers, of which five have been settled and four remain in litigation. The five settled cases resulted in disgorgements ranging from $2,736 to $7.05 million, civil penalties ranging from $8,208 to $4.7 million, a suspension, and bars from the securities industry.

According to an SEC enforcement official, SEC recognized that hedge funds were becoming a prominent force in the financial industry, and in anticipation that certain hedge fund advisers would be required to register with SEC as investment advisers when the now vacated amendment to Rule 203(b)(3)-1 was under consideration, SEC created a hedge fund working group composed primarily of Enforcement and Office of Compliance Inspections and Examinations staff and participants from other divisions. The goals of this group are to enhance SEC's staff knowledge about the hedge fund industry to aid in its oversight role and coordinate and strengthen the agency's efforts to combat insider trading at hedge funds. Currently, SEC is conducting investigations into potential insider trading by hedge fund advisers.

SEC Monitors Risk Management Practices at the Largest Securities Firms with Significant Hedge Fund Activities

SEC also conducts oversight over hedge fund activities through the supervision of the regulated securities firms that transact business with hedge funds as brokers, creditors, and counterparties. SEC staff oversees some large, internationally active U.S. securities firms with significant hedge fund activities through its Consolidated Supervised Entity program (CSE), which was established in June 2004.[30] Between December 2004 and November 2005, five large securities firms have elected to become CSEs.[31] The CSE program consists of four components: (1) a review of the firm's application to become a CSE; (2) a review of monthly, quarterly, and annual filings, such as consolidated financial statements and risk reports, substantially similar to those provided to the firm's senior management; (3) monthly meetings with senior management (senior risk managers and financial controllers) at the holding company level to review financial and risk reports and share written results of these meetings among staff and commissioners; and (4) an examination of books and records of the ultimate holding company, the broker-dealer, and material affiliates.[32] SEC relies on a number of regulatory tools, including margin, capital, and reporting requirements to oversee CSEs. Margin rules within the broker- dealer help protect against losses resulting from defaults by requiring its hedge fund clients to provide collateral in amounts that depend on the risk of the particular position and help maintain safety and soundness of their firms. Capital requirements are minimum regulatory required levels of capital that a firm must hold against its risk-taking activities. These requirements can help a firm withstand the failure of a counterparty or a period of market or systemic stress.

One aspect of the CSE program involves how the securities firms manage various risk exposures, including those from hedge fund activities such as providing prime brokerage service and acting as creditors and counterparties through financing and OTC derivatives trade transactions. These large integrated financial institutions may be exposed to various risks from hedge fund activities such as providing prime brokerage services through a registered broker-dealer, acting as creditors and counterparties, or owning a hedge fund. For example, the recent problems at two hedge funds sponsored by Bear Stearns Asset Management that invested in financial instruments tied to subprime mortgages (where Bear Stearns ultimately provided some secured financing to the funds) highlight such risks. As part of the application process that took place from November 2004 through January 2006, SEC examined the five securities firms' risk management systems (market, credit, liquidity, operational, and legal and compliance), internal controls, and capital adequacy calculations and continues to do so on an ongoing basis. SEC did not target hedge fund activities specifically within the scope of the five application examinations, because hedge funds were not products or activities judged to pose the greatest risks to the firms. Our review of the five CSEs' application examinations found that examination findings generally were related to firms' documentation of compliance with rules and requirements. SEC shared the findings with the firms and has monitored the firms' implementation of its recommendations. An SEC official said that those issues have been resolved, but more recently, SEC's examinations of three of the firms identified a number of issues related to capital computations, operational controls, and risk management. Examination staff are addressing these issues with the firms.

SEC monitors CSEs continuously for financial and operational weakness that might place regulated entities within the group or the broader financial system at risk. According to an SEC official, the CSE program allows SEC to conduct reviews across the five firms (i.e., cross-firm reviews) to gain insights into business areas that are material by risk or balance sheet measures, rapidly growing, pose particular challenges in implementing the Basel regulatory risk-based capital regime, or have some combination of these characteristics.[33] For example, in fiscal year 2006, SEC conducted two cross-firm reviews related to leveraged lending and hedge fund derivatives, and in fiscal year 2007, SEC conducted two cross- firm reviews related to securitization and private equity and principal investments.[34] According to the official, SEC generally found that the firms were in regulatory compliance, but there were areas where capital computation methodology and risk management practices can be improved. For example, four firms modified their capital computations as a result of feedback from the leveraged lending project. For each review, SEC produced a report that described the business model, related risk management, and capital treatment to each review area, and provided feedback to each firm on where it stood among the peer firms.

CFTC Can Monitor Hedge Fund Activities through Its Market Surveillance, Regulatory Compliance Surveillance, and Delegated Examination Programs

Although CFTC does not specifically target hedge funds, through its general market and financial supervisory activities, it can provide oversight of persons registered as CPOs and CTAs that operate or advise hedge funds that trade in the futures markets. As part of its market surveillance program, CFTC collects information on market participants, regardless of their registration status, to monitor their activities and trading practices. In particular, traders are required to report their futures and options positions when a CFTC-specified level is reached in a certain contract market and CFTC electronically collects these data through its Large Trader Reporting System (LTRS).[35] CFTC also uses the futures and options positions information reported by traders through the LTRS as part of its monitoring of the potential financial exposure of traders to clearing firms, and of clearing firms to derivatives clearing organizations. CFTC collects position information from exchanges, clearing members, futures commission merchants (FCM), and foreign brokers and other traders—including hedge funds—about firm and customer accounts in an attempt to detect and deter manipulation.[36] Customers, including hedge funds, are required to maintain margin on deposit with their FCMs to cover losses that might be incurred due to price changes. FCMs also are required to maintain CFTC-imposed minimum capital requirements in order to meet their financial obligations. Such financial safeguards are put in place to mitigate the potential spillover effect to the broader market resulting from the failure of a customer or of an FCM.

According to CFTC officials, the demise (due to trading losses related to natural gas derivatives) in the fall of 2006 of Amaranth Advisors, LLC (Amaranth), a $9 billion multistrategy hedge fund, had no impact on the integrity of the clearing system for CFTC-regulated futures and option contracts. The officials said that at all times Amaranth's account at its clearing FCM was fully margined and the clearing FCM met all of its settlement obligations to its clearinghouse. They also said that the approximate $6 billion of losses suffered by Amaranth on regulated and unregulated exchanges did not affect its clearing FCM, the other customers of the clearing FCM, or the clearinghouse.[37]

CFTC investigates and, as necessary, prosecutes alleged violators of the Commodity Exchange Act (CEA) and CFTC regulations and may conduct such investigations in cooperation with federal, state, and foreign authorities.

Enforcement referrals can come from several sources, including CFTC's market surveillance group or tips. Remedies sought in enforcement actions generally include permanent injunctions, asset freezes, prohibitions on trading on CFTC-registered entities, disgorgement of ill-gotten gains, restitution to victims, revocation or suspension of registration, and civil monetary penalties. On the basis of CFTC enforcement data, from the beginning of fiscal year 2001 through May 1, 2007, CFTC brought 58 enforcement actions against CPOs and CTAs, including those affiliated with hedge funds, for various violations.[38] A summary of the violations cited in the actions includes misrepresentation with respect to assets under management or profitability; failure to register with CFTC; failure to make required disclosures, statement, or reports; misappropriation of participants' funds; and violation of prior prohibitions (i.e., prior civil injunction or CFTC cease and desist order).

Pursuant to CFTC-delegated authority, NFA, a registered futures association under the CEA and a self-regulatory organization, oversees the activities, and conducts examinations, of registered CPOs and CTAs.[39] As such, hedge fund advisers registered as CPOs or CTAs are subject to direct oversight in connection with their trading in futures markets.[40] More specifically, to the extent that hedge fund operators or advisers trade futures or options on futures on behalf of hedge funds, the funds are commodity pools and the operators of, and advisers to, such funds are required to register as CPOs and CTAs, respectively, with CFTC and become members of NFA if they are not exempted from registration. Once registered, CPOs and CTAs become subject to detailed disclosure, periodic reporting and record-keeping requirements, and periodic on-site risk- based examinations. However, regardless of registration status, all CPOs and CTAs (including those affiliated with hedge funds) remain subject to CFTC's anti-fraud and anti-manipulation authority.

Our review of NFA documentation found that 29 advisers of the largest 78 U.S. hedge funds (previously mentioned) are registered with CFTC as CPOs or CTAs. In addition, 20 of the 29 also are registered with SEC as investment advisers or broker-dealers. According to NFA officials, because there is no legal definition of hedge funds, it does not require CPOs or CTAs to identify themselves as hedge fund operators or advisers. NFA, therefore, considers all CPOs and CTAs as potential hedge fund operators or advisers. According to NFA, in fiscal year 2006 NFA examined 212 CPOs, including 6 of the 29 largest hedge fund advisers registered with NFA. During the examinations, NFA staff performed tests of books and records and other auditing procedures to provide reasonable assurance that the firm was complying with NFA rules and all account balances of a certain date were properly stated and classified. Our review of four of the examinations found that 3 of the CPOs examined generally were in compliance with NFA regulations and the remaining 1 was found to have certain employees that were not properly registered with CFTC. According to examination documentation, subsequent to the examination, the hedge fund provided a satisfactory written response to NFA noting that it would soon properly register the employees.

According to an NFA official, since 2003 NFA has taken 23 enforcement actions against CPOs and CTAs, many of which involved hedge funds. Some of the violations found included filing fraudulent financial statements with NFA, not providing timely financial statements to investors, failure to register with CFTC as a CPO, failure to maintain required books and records, use of misleading promotional materials, and failure to supervise staff. The penalties included barring CPOs and CTAs from NFA membership temporarily or permanently or imposing monetary fines ranging from $5,000 to $45,000.

Bank Regulators Have Conducted Some Examinations Relating to Hedge Fund Business at Banks

Bank regulators (the Federal Reserve, OCC, and FDIC) monitor the risk management practices of their regulated institutions' interactions with hedge funds as creditors and counterparties. They are responsible for ensuring that the organizations under their jurisdiction are complying with supervisory guidance and industry sound practices regarding prudent risk management throughout their business, including the guidance and practices applicable to their activities with hedge funds. The 1999 PWG report recommended that bank regulators encourage improvements in the risk management systems of the regulated entities and promote the development of a more risk-based approach to capital adequacy.

In overseeing banks' hedge fund-related activities, the bank regulators examine the extent to which banks are following sound practices as part of their reviews of banks' capital market activities. Bank regulators conduct routine supervisory examinations of risk management practices relating to hedge funds and other highly leveraged counterparties to ensure that the supervised entities (1) perform appropriate due diligence in assessing the business, risk exposures, and credit standing of their counterparties; (2) establish, monitor, and enforce appropriate quantitative risk exposure limits for each of their counterparties; (3) use appropriate systems to identify, measure, and manage counterparty credit risk; and (4) deploy appropriate internal controls to ensure the integrity of their processes for managing counterparty credit risk.

The Federal Reserve's supervision of banks' hedge fund-related activities is part of a broader, more comprehensive set of supervisory initiatives to assess whether banks' risk management practices and financial market infrastructures are sufficiently robust to cope with stresses that could accompany deteriorating market conditions. Specifically, the Federal Reserve has been focusing on five key supervisory initiatives: (1) comprehensive reviews of firms' corporate-level stress testing practices, (2) a multilateral supervisory assessment of the leading global banks' current practices for managing their exposures to hedge funds, (3) a review of the risks associated with the rapid growth of leveraged lending, (4) a new assessment of practices to manage liquidity risk, and (5) continued efforts to reduce risks associated with weaknesses in the clearing and settlement of credit derivatives and other OTC derivatives.

The bank regulators also have performed targeted examinations of the credit risk management practices of regulated entities that are major hedge fund creditors or counterparties. From 2004 through 2007, FRBNY conducted various reviews that addressed aspects of certain banks' counterparty credit risk management practices that involved hedge fund activities. These reviews were motivated by the rapid growth of the hedge fund industry and also done to gauge progress made in improving risk management practices pursuant to supervisory guidance and industry recommendations. Examiners conducted meetings with management and reviewed policies and procedures primarily by performing transactional testing, relying on internal audits, and studying other functional regulators' reviews.

According to a Federal Reserve official, while global banks have significantly strengthened their risk management practices and procedures for managing risk exposures to hedge funds, further progress is needed. For example, in a 2006 firmwide examination of stress-testing practices at certain U.S. banks, FRBNY indicated a need for the banks "to enhance their capacity to aggregate credit exposures at the firm wide level, including across counterparties; to assess the potential for counterparty credit losses to be compounded by losses on the banks' proprietary trading positions; and to assess the potential effects of a rapid and possibly a protracted decline in asset market liquidity."[41] According to this official, the Federal Reserve has begun a review of liquidity risk management practices at the largest U.S. bank holding companies, focusing on the firms' efforts to ensure adequate funding in more adverse market conditions.[42]

Federal Reserve examiners made a variety of other recommendations as a result of the various reviews. Many of their recommendations were developed as ways that banks could continue to enhance their risk management processes associated with hedge fund counterparties. The examiners found a range of practices for counterparty stress testing for hedge funds and noted that there was room for improvement even at the banks with the most advanced practices. Where examiners identified deficiencies, specific recommendations were made. Although credit officers often adjusted credit terms for degree of transparency, examiners recommended that banks' policies explicitly link transparency to credit terms and that banks monitor evolving credit terms for hedge fund counterparties. Moreover, examiners found that the banks that were part of the reviews needed to enhance their policies to more specifically address due diligence requirements or standards to provide clearer standards and guidance for reviewing hedge fund valuation processes.

In 2005 and 2006, OCC conducted an examination of hedge fund-related activities—mainly counterparty credit risk management practices (such as due diligence of their hedge fund customer's business), and margining and collateral monitoring processes—at the three large U.S. banks. OCC generally found the overall risk management practices of these banks to be satisfactory. However, examiners identified concerns in the lack of transparency in the banks' hedge fund review processes and issued recommendations accordingly. For example, examiners found in certain banks a lack of adequate credit review policies that clearly outline risk assessment criteria for levels of leverage, risk strategies and concentrations, and other key parameters and documentation to support accuracy of a bank's credit analysis and risk rating system. Examiners also found that financial information provided by some hedge fund borrowers has been incomplete and that banks should document the lack of such information in their credit review process. OCC noted that the banks have taken satisfactory steps in response to examination issues raised.

In addition, in 2005 and 2006, FDIC conducted an examination of hedge fund lending at one of its banks. FDIC noted that the bank was not in compliance with the bank's lending policy to diversify its hedge fund loans and that certain policies should be updated, but generally found the risk management practices of the bank's hedge fund lending program to be satisfactory.

Bank regulators largely rely on their oversight of hedge fund-related activities at those regulated entities that transact with hedge funds in their efforts to mitigate the potential for hedge funds to contribute to systemic risk. Since 2004, regulators have increased their attention to these activities. In particular, bank regulators are reviewing the entities' ability to identify and manage their counterparty credit risk exposures, including those that involve hedge funds. Regulated entities have the responsibility to practice prudent risk management standards, but prudent standards do not guarantee prudent practices. As such, it will be important for regulators to show continued vigilance in overseeing banks' hedge fund- related activities.

In: Hedge Funds: Regulation and Nonregulation ISBN: 978-1-60692-041-1
Editor: Yeram E. Torrey, pp. 27-33 © 2009 Nova Science Publishers, Inc.

Chapter 4

INVESTORS, CREDITORS, AND COUNTERPARTIES HAVE INCREASED EFFORTS TO IMPOSE DISCIPLINE ON HEDGE FUND ADVISERS, BUT SOME LIMITATIONS REMAIN

Investors, creditors, and counterparties impose market discipline—by rewarding well-managed hedge funds and reducing their exposure to risky, poorly managed hedge funds—during due diligence exercises and through ongoing monitoring. During due diligence, hedge funds should be asked to provide credible information about risks and prospective returns. Market participants told us that growing investments by institutional investors with fiduciary responsibilities and guidance from regulators and industry groups led hedge fund advisers to improve disclosure and transparency in recent years. Creditors and counterparties also can impose market discipline through ongoing management of credit terms (such as collateral requirements). However, some market participants and regulators identified limitations to market discipline or failures to exercise it properly. For instance, large hedge funds use multiple prime brokers, making it unlikely that any single broker would have all the data needed to assess a client's total leverage. Others were concerned that some creditors and counterparties may lack the capacity to assess risk exposures because of the complex financial instruments and investment strategies that some hedge funds use, which could illustrate a failure to exercise market discipline properly if the creditor or counterparty continued to do business with the fund. Further, regulators have raised concerns that creditors may have relaxed credit standards to attract and retain hedge fund clients, another potential failure of market discipline.

Better due Diligence and Greater Demand for Transparency from Investors Have Resulted in Increased Hedge Fund Disclosure, but Some Investors May Lack the Capacity to Assess Risk Exposures

By evaluating hedge fund management, the fund's business activities, and its internal controls, investors are imposing discipline on hedge fund advisers. Market participants who generally transact with large hedge funds and institutional investors told us that before investing in a hedge fund, potential investors usually conduct a due diligence exercise of the business, management, legal, and operational aspects of the hedge fund under consideration for investment. Market participants further noted that the exercise moves from an initial screening to quickly identify the funds that do meet the potential investor's investment criteria to a detailed evaluation that involves addressing a series of questions about the business, management, legal, and operational aspects of the hedge fund. Among other things, investors may take into account investment strategies hedge funds use to produce their returns, the types of investments traded, and the fund's risk management practices and risk profiles. Investors analyze this information to determine whether the investment's risks and reward warrant further consideration.

Typically, prospective investors receive written information from the hedge fund manager in the form of a private offering memorandum or private placement memorandum (PPM).[43] We could not obtain hedge fund offering documents, but market participants who have reviewed PPMs told us that there are no standard disclosure requirements for PPMs and the information disclosed is often general in scope. Consequently, investors may seek information beyond that provided in PPMs and sometimes beyond what hedge funds are willing to provide. For instance, they may request from hedge fund managers a list of hedge fund securities positions and holdings (position transparency) or information about the risks associated with the hedge fund's market positions (risk transparency).

However, according to market participants we interviewed, although most hedge funds may be willing to provide information on aggregate position and holdings, many hedge funds decline to share specific position transparency, citing the need to keep such information confidential for fear that disclosure might permit other market participants to take advantage of their trading positions to the detriment of the fund and its investors. Additionally, some prospective investors also may obtain from hedge fund managers access to the hedge funds' prime brokers and other service providers such as auditors, lawyers, fund administrators, and accountants for background checks. A representative of a group that represents institutional investors we met with told us that after making an investment, investors typically will monitor their investment on an ongoing basis to evaluate portfolio performance and track how well investments are moving toward investment goals and benchmarks.

Recently, hedge fund advisers have increased their level of disclosure in response to demands from institutional investors. Institutional investments in hedge funds have grown substantially in recent years. Over the last 3 years, institutional investors in search of higher returns and risk diversification, such as pension funds, endowments, and funds of hedge funds, have accounted for a significant portion of the inflows to hedge funds assets under management. (See app. II for information on pension plan investments in hedge funds). According to market participants and industry literature, the increasing popularity of hedge funds among these institutional investors has led to changes in the industry. That is, hedge fund advisers have responded to the requirements of these clients by providing disclosure that allows them to meet fiduciary responsibilities. For example, one market participant we met with stated that a trustee to a pension plan that is subject to the "prudent person" standard of the Employee Retirement Income Security Act of 1974 (ERISA) is required to make investment decisions for the plan in accordance with a "prudent person" standard of care that may require plan trustees to demand greater quality oversight of their capital; in consequence, they may demand greater transparency, risk information, and valuation techniques than individual investors.[44] Market participants with whom we met also told us that the trend toward permanent capital also has been driving hedge fund transparency. Markets participants further noted that as hedge funds reach a certain size, they tend to seek more permanent capital through the public markets to avoid the liquidity risks inherent with sudden investor redemptions.

The ability of market discipline to control hedge funds' risk taking is limited by some investors' inability to fully understand and evaluate the information they receive on hedge fund activities or these investors' willingness to hire others to evaluate that information for them. An example can be found in the Amaranth case. According to market participants we interviewed and industry coverage that documented the event, Amaranth noted in its periodic letters to investors that it had a large concentration in the natural gas sector. The market participants and the documents noted that some investors became concerned about the potential risks associated with concentrated positions and withdrew their money from Amaranth several months before Amaranth failed. They also said that other investors did not heed potential warning signs included in the investor letter and kept their money in Amaranth either in pursuit of higher investment returns or because they did not fully comprehend the changing risk profile of the hedge fund.

Regulators, market participants, and academics generally agree that hedge funds have improved disclosure and risk management practices since the LTCM crisis and have largely adopted the guidance from various industry groups and the PWG. Regulators told us that from their examinations of regulated entities that transact business with hedge funds as creditors and counterparties, they have observed that hedge fund disclosure and risk management practices have improved since LTCM. For example, in response to the 1999 PWG report recommendation that hedge funds establish a set of sound practices for risk management and internal controls, private sector entities such as the Managed Funds Association (MFA), and the Counterparty Risk Management Policy Group (CRMPG), as well as the public sector International Organization of Securities Commissions (IOSCO) published guidance for hedge funds and their advisers.[45] Market participants told us that many hedge fund advisers with which they conduct business have adopted these best practices, including risk management models that go beyond measuring "value at risk," and now regularly stress-test portfolios under a wide range of adverse conditions.[46] Representatives from a risk management firm told us that in the past, hedge fund advisers viewed risk management practices as proprietary. However, as the trading environment evolved, advisers realized they needed to provide results of risk assessments to investors to attract investments.

Creditors and Counterparties Can Impose Some Market Discipline on Hedge Fund Advisers as Part of Credit Extension, but the Complexity of Counterparty Credit Risk Management Poses Ongoing Challenges for Financial Institutions

By evaluating hedge fund management, the fund's business activities, and its internal and risk management controls, creditors and counterparties exert discipline on hedge fund advisers. According to market participants, entering into contracts with hedge funds as creditors or counterparties is the primary mechanism by which financial institutions' credit exposures to hedge funds arise, and exercising counterparty risk management is the primary mechanism by which financial institutions impose market discipline on hedge funds. According to the staff of the member agencies of the PWG, the credit risk exposures between hedge funds and their creditors and counterparties arise primarily from trading and lending relationships, including various types of derivatives and securities transactions.[47] As part of the credit extension process, creditors and counterparties typically require hedge funds to post collateral that can be sold in the event of default. According to market participants we interviewed, collateral most often takes the form of cash or high-quality, highly liquid securities (e.g., government securities), but it can also include lower-rated securities (e.g., BBB rated bonds) and less liquid assets (e.g., CDOs). They told us they take steps to ensure that they have clear control over collateral that is pledged, which according to some creditors and counterparties we interviewed, that was not the case with LTCM.

Creditors and counterparties generally require hedge funds to post collateral to cover current credit exposures (this generally occurs daily) and, with some exceptions, require additional collateral, or initial margin, to cover potential exposures that could arise if markets moved sharply.[48] Creditors to hedge funds said that they measure a fund's current and potential risk exposure on a daily basis to evaluate counterparty positions and collateral.

To control their risk exposures, creditors and counterparties to generally large hedge funds told us that, unlike in the late 1990s, they now conduct more extensive due diligence and ongoing monitoring of a hedge fund client. According to OCC, banks also conduct "abbreviated" underwriting procedures for small hedge funds in which they do not conduct much due diligence. OCC officials also told us that losses due to the extension of credit to hedge funds were rare. Creditors and counterparties of large hedge funds use their own internal rating and credit or counterparty risk management process and may require additional collateral from hedge funds as a buffer against increased risk exposure. They said that as part of their due diligence, they typically request information that includes hedge fund managers' background and track record; risk measures; periodic net asset valuation calculations; side pockets and side letters; fees and redemption policy; liquidity, valuations, capital measures, and net changes to capital; and annual audited statements. According to industry and regulatory officials familiar with the LTCM episode, this was not necessarily the case in the 1990s. At that time, creditors and counterparties had not asked enough questions about the risks that were being taken to generate the high returns. Creditors and counterparties told us they currently establish credit terms partly based on the scope and depth of information that hedge funds are willing to provide, the willingness of the fund managers to answer questions during on-site visits, and the assessment of the hedge fund's risk exposure and capacity to manage risk. If approved, the hedge fund receives a credit rating and a line of credit. Several prime brokers told us that losses from hedge fund clients were extremely rare due to the asset-based lending they provided such funds. Also, one prime broker noted that during the course of its monitoring the risk profile of a hedge fund client, it noticed that the hedge fund manager was taking what the broker considered to be excessive risk, and requested additional information on the fund's activity. The client did not comply with the prime broker's request for additional information, and the prime broker terminated the relationship with the client.

Through continuous monitoring of counterparty credit exposure to hedge funds, creditors and counterparties can further impose market discipline on hedge fund advisers. Some creditors and counterparties also told us that they measure counterparty credit exposure on an ongoing basis through a credit system that is updated each day to determine current and potential exposures. Credit officers at one bank said that they receive monthly investor summaries from many of their hedge fund clients. The summaries provide information for monitoring the activities and performance of hedge funds. Officials at another bank told us that they generally monitor their hedge fund clients on a quarterly basis and may alter credit terms or terminate a relationship if it is determined that the fund is not dealing with risk adequately or if it does not disclose requested information.

Some creditors also said that they may provide better credit terms to hedge funds that consolidate all trade executions and settlements at their firm than to hedge funds that use several prime brokers because they would know more about the fund's exposure. However, large hedge funds may limit the information they provide to banks and prime brokers for various reasons. Unlike small hedge funds that generally depend on a single prime broker for a large number of services ranging from capital introductions to the generation of customized accounting reports, many large hedge funds are less dependent on the services of any single prime broker and, according to several market participants, use multiple prime brokers as a means to protect proprietary trading positions and strategies, and to diversify their credit and operational risks.

Despite improvements in disclosure and counterparty credit risk management, regulators noted that the effectiveness of market discipline may be limited or market discipline may not be exercised properly for several reasons. First, because large hedge funds use several prime brokers as creditors and counterparties, no single prime broker may be able to assess the total amount of leverage used by a large hedge fund client. The stress tests and other tools that prime brokers use to monitor a given counterparty's risk profile can incorporate only those positions known to a trading partner. Second, the increasing complexity of structured financial instruments has raised concerns that counterparties lack the capacity (in terms of risk models and resources) to keep pace with and assess actual risk, illustrating a possible failure to exercise market discipline properly. More specifically, despite improvements in risk modeling and risk management, the Federal Reserve believes that further progress is needed in the procedures global banks use to manage exposures to highly leveraged counterparties such as hedge funds, in part because of the increasing complexity of products such as structured credit products and CDOs in which hedge funds are active participants. The complexity of structured credit products can add to the already complex task of measuring and managing counterparty credit risk. For example, another Federal Reserve official has noted that the measurement of counterparty credit risk requires complex computer simulations and that "the management of counterparty risk is also complicated further by hedge funds' complicated organizational structures, legal rights, collateral arrangements, and frequent trading. It is important that banks develop the systems capability to regularly gather and analyze data across diverse internal systems to manage their counterparty credit risk to hedge funds." One regulatory official further noted the challenges faced by institutions in finding, developing and retaining individuals with the expertise required to analyze the adequacy of these increasingly complex models. The lack of talented staff can affect counterparty credit risk monitoring and the ability to impose market discipline on hedge fund risk taking activities. Third, some regulators have expressed concerns that some creditors and counterparties may have relaxed their counterparty credit risk management practices for hedge funds, which could weaken the effectiveness of market discipline as a tool to limit the exposure of hedge fund managers. They noted that competition for hedge fund clients may have led some to reduce the initial margin in collateral agreements, reducing the amount of collateral to cover potential credit exposure.

In: Hedge Funds: Regulation and Nonregulation ISBN: 978-1-60692-041-1
Editor: Yeram E. Torrey, pp. 35-41 © 2009 Nova Science Publishers, Inc.

Chapter 5

REGULATORS VIEW HEDGE FUND ACTIVITIES AS POTENTIAL SOURCES OF SYSTEMIC RISK AND ARE TAKING MEASURES TO ENHANCE MARKET DISCIPLINE AND PREPARE FOR FINANCIAL DISRUPTIONS

Financial regulators and industry observers remain concerned about the adequacy of counterparty credit risk management at major financial institutions because it is a key factor in controlling the potential for hedge funds to become a source of systemic risk. While hedge funds generally add liquidity to many markets, including distressed asset markets, in some circumstances hedge funds' activities can strain liquidity and contribute to financial distress. In response to their concerns regarding the adequacy of counterparty credit risk, a group of regulators have, over the past year, been collaborating to examine particular hedge fund-related activities across entities they regulate, mainly through international multilateral efforts and the domestic PWG. The PWG also has established two private sector committees to identify best practices to address systemic risk and investor protection issues and has formalized protocols to respond to financial shocks.

Despite Intensified Market Discipline, Concerns about Hedge Funds Creating Systemic Risk Remain

Financial regulators believe that the market discipline imposed by investors, creditors, and counterparties is the most effective mechanism for limiting the systemic risk from the activities of hedge funds (and other private pools of capital). The most important providers of market discipline are the large, global commercial and investment banks that are hedge funds' principal creditors and counterparties. While regulators and others recognize that counterparty credit risk management has improved since LTCM, the ability of financial institutions to maintain the adequacy of these management processes in light of the dramatic growth in hedge fund activities remains a particular focus of concern. In its July 2005 report, CRMPG noted that "credit risk and, in particular counterparty credit risk, is probably the single most important variable in determining whether and with what speed financial disturbances become financial shocks with potential systemic traits."[49] CRMPG further noted that no single hedge fund today is leveraged on a scale comparable to that of LTCM in 1998 and that the risk management capabilities of hedge funds had improved. Although CRMPG concluded that the chance of systemic financial shocks had declined, Treasury officials noted that regulators continually review whether the failure of one or more large market participants, including hedge funds, could destabilize regulated financial institutions or financial markets in a way that generates broader macroeconomic consequences.[50]

Effective market discipline requires that the creditors and counterparties to hedge funds obtain sufficient information to reliably assess clients' risk profiles and that they have systems to monitor and limit exposures to levels commensurate with each client's risk and creditworthiness. A number of large commercial banks and prime brokers bear and manage the credit and counterparty risks that hedge fund leverage creates. According to a Federal Reserve official, the recent growth of hedge funds poses formidable challenges, including significant risk management challenges to these market participants. If market participants prove unwilling or unable to meet these challenges, losses in the hedge fund sector could pose significant risk to financial stability. Concerns remain that creditors and counterparties face constant challenges in measuring and managing counterparty credit risk exposures to hedge funds, and in maintaining qualified staff to implement the various elements of counterparty credit risk management, including stress testing.

In addition to counterparty credit risk, Treasury officials noted that regulators continually review the liquidity of markets to determine whether the trading behavior of market participants, including hedge funds, could serve as a source of systemic risk. While hedge funds often provide liquidity to stressed markets by buying securities that are temporarily distressed, herding behavior by market participants, including hedge funds, could strain available market liquidity. According to a Treasury official, "If numerous market participants establish large positions on the same side of a trade, especially in combination with a high degree of leverage, this concentration can contribute to a liquidity crisis if market conditions compel traders to simultaneously unwind their positions. "[51] Some market participants noted that the consequences of these "crowded" trades were difficult to anticipate.

Some Federal Reserve officials noted in a journal article that "in a crisis, interlocking credit exposures would be the key mechanism by which risks would be transmitted from one institution to another, potentially transforming a run-of-the-mill disturbance into a systematic situation."[52] The forced sale of assets is recognized by regulators as a potential transmission mechanism for systemic risk. According to these officials, regulators in general share concerns that "in illiquid markets, hedge funds may be forced to sell positions to meet margin requirements, driving down market prices. In severe cases, the hedge fund may drive down the value of existing positions by more than they receive from the original sale, forcing further sales."[53] However, this transmission mechanism is not unique to hedge funds but is a characteristic of leverage. Even when the failure of a hedge fund does not result in a large-scale liquidation of assets, the concerns raised by the failure can disrupt credit markets. For instance, concerns regarding the valuation of illiquid subprime mortgages, such as those held by Bear Stearns Asset Management's hedge funds, have contributed to questions about credit quality in this and other markets, and this broader questioning of credit quality may have contributed to the subsequent tightening of credit.[54]

Regulators Are Taking Steps to Strengthen Market Discipline to Address Systemic Risk Concerns Stemming from Hedge Fund Activities

To enhance market discipline and help mitigate the potential systemic risks that hedge fund activities could pose, financial regulators recently have increased collaboration with each other, foreign financial regulators, and industry participants. They have been conducting these efforts primarily through an international review of large financial institutions and actions initiated by the PWG. As discussed earlier, hedge funds are a potential source of systemic risk if the capacity of their creditors and counterparties to value positions and manage risk does not keep pace with developments such as the increasing complexity of financial instruments and of investment strategies. Because the use of these instruments and strategies is not exclusive to hedge funds, a regulator said that collecting data on hedge fund activities to monitor buildup of this risk would be difficult and not meaningful. Instead, regulators have taken a risk-focused and principles-based approach by monitoring counterparty risk management practices across regulated entities and issuing guidance to help strengthen market discipline. Currently, regulators are reviewing issues related to the valuation of complex, illiquid, and stressed instruments by all types of entities. The PWG has also formalized protocols for coordination among the financial regulators in the event of a financial market crisis.

In late 2006, FRBNY, SEC, OCC, FSA, and bank regulators of Germany and Switzerland—collectively, the "multilateral effort"—jointly conducted a review of the largest commercial and investment banks that transacted business with hedge funds as counterparties and creditors. The agencies met with nine major U.S. and European bank and securities firms to discuss risk management policies and procedures related to interactions with hedge funds through prime brokerage, direct lending, and over-the- counter derivative transactions. According to one U.S. regulator, the reviewers found that the current and potential credit exposures of these banks to hedge funds were small relative to the banks' capital because of their extensive use of collateral agreements. However, the reviewers identified a number of issues related to the management of exposures to hedge funds and the measurement of potential exposures in adverse market conditions. The regulators participating in this effort have been addressing these issues by gathering additional data or information to help regulators learn more about the condition and quality of the firms' risk management practices. The regulators are conducting an ongoing follow- up review, which entails more detailed work by the principal regulator of each firm.

In February 2007, the PWG issued principles-based guidance for approaching issues related to private pools of capital, including hedge funds. The principles are intended to guide market participants (for example, hedge fund advisers, creditors, counterparties, and investors), as well as U.S. financial regulators as they address investor protection and systemic risk issues associated with the rapid growth of private pools of capital and the complexity of financial instruments and investment strategies they employ. The efforts for each group of stakeholders enumerated in the principles and guidelines that the PWG issued entitled "Agreement Among PWG and U.S. Agency Principals on Principles and Guidelines Regarding Private Pools of Capital" are briefly summarized below:

- "**Private Pools of Capital:** maintain and enhance information, valuation, and risk management systems to provide market participants with accurate, sufficient, and timely information.
- **Investors:** consider the suitability of investments in a private pool in light of investment objectives, risk tolerances, and the principle of portfolio diversification.
- **Counterparties and Creditors:** commit sufficient resources to maintain and enhance risk management practices.
- **Regulators and Supervisors:** work together to communicate and use authority to ensure that supervisory expectations regarding counterparty risk management practices and market integrity are met."

The PWG's principles and guidelines are intended to enhance market discipline, which the PWG stated most effectively addresses systemic risk posed by private pools of capital, without deterring the benefits such pools of capital provide to the U.S. economy. According to a Treasury official involved in developing the PWG guidance, the PWG believes that self- interested, more sophisticated, informed investors, creditors, and counterparties have their own economic incentives to take actions to reduce and manage their own risks, which will reduce systemic risk overall and enhance investor protection. Also, the PWG continues to believe that regulators have an important role to play in addressing these issues.

Further, in September 2007, the PWG established two private sector committees. One committee comprised asset managers, and the other comprised investors, including labor organizations, endowments, foundations, corporate and public pension funds, investment consultants, and other U.S. and non-U.S. investors. The first task of these committees will be to develop best practices using the PWG's principles-based guidance released in February 2007 as a foundation to enhance investor protection and systemic risk safeguards. According to the mission statement of the asset managers' committee, best practices will cover asset advisers having information, valuation, and risk management systems that meet sound industry practices. In turn, these systems would enable them to provide accurate information to creditors, counterparties, and investors with appropriate frequency, breadth, and detail. According to the mission statement of the investors' committee, best practices would cover information, due diligence, risk management, and reporting and build on the PWG guidelines related to disclosure, due diligence, risk management capabilities, the suitability of the strategies of private pools given an investor's risk tolerance, and fiduciary duties. According to staff of the PWG member agencies, the PWG expects both committees to have drafts of the best practices available for public comment early in 2008 and to issue final products in the spring.

Finally, recognizing that financial shocks are inevitable, the PWG told us that it adopted more formalized protocols in fall 2006 to coordinate communications among the appropriate regulatory bodies in the event of market turmoil, including a liquidity crisis. The protocols include a detailed list of contact information for domestic and international regulatory bodies, financial institutions, risk managers, and traders, and procedures for communications. According to staff of the PWG member agencies, the protocols were used to handle recent events such as the fallout from the Amaranth losses in 2006 and the losses from subprime mortgage investments by two Bear Stearns hedge funds in summer 2007.

Addressing potential systemic risk posed by hedge fund activities involves actions by investors, creditors and counterparties, hedge fund advisers, and regulators. The regulators and the PWG's recent initiatives are intended to bring together these various groups to improve current practices related to hedge fund-related activities and to better prepare for a potential financial crisis. We view these initiatives as positive steps taken to address systemic risk. However, it is too soon to evaluate their effectiveness.

AGENCY COMMENTS

We provided a draft of this report to CFTC, DOL, Federal Reserve, FDIC, OCC, OTS, SEC, and Treasury for their review and comment. None of the agencies provided written comments. All except for FDIC and OTS provided technical comments, which we have incorporated into the report as appropriate.

As agreed with your offices, unless you publicly announce its contents earlier, we plan no further distribution of this report until 30 days after the date of this report. At that time, we will send copies of this report to the Ranking Member of the Committee on Financial Services, House of Representatives; the Chairman and Ranking Member of the Committee on Banking, Housing, and Urban Affairs, U.S. Senate; Ranking Member of the Subcommittee on Capital Markets, Insurance and Government Sponsored Enterprises, House of Representatives; and other interested congressional committees. We are also sending copies to the Chairman, Board of Governors of the Federal Reserve System; Chairman,

Commodity Futures Trading Commission; Chairman, Federal Deposit Insurance Corporation; Secretary of Labor; Comptroller of the Currency, Office of the Comptroller of the Currency; Director, Office of Thrift Supervision; Chairman, Securities and Exchange Commission; Secretary of the Treasury; and other interested parties. We will make copies available to others upon request. The report will also be available at no charge on our Web site at http://www.gao.gov.

If you or your staff have any questions regarding this report, please contact me at (202) 512-8678 or williamso@gao.gov. Contact points for our Office of Congressional Relations and Public Affairs may be found on the last page of this report. GAO staff who made major contributions to this report are listed in appendix IY.

Orice M. Williams
Director, Financial Markets and Community Investment

In: Hedge Funds: Regulation and Nonregulation ISBN: 978-1-60692-041-1
Editor: Yeram E. Torrey, pp. 43-45 © 2009 Nova Science Publishers, Inc.

APPENDIX I: SCOPE AND METHODOLOGY

To address the first objective (regulatory oversight of hedge fund-related activities), we reviewed regulatory examination documents (for example, examination modules, scoping, examination reports and findings, corrective actions taken or proposed by firms, and regulatory follow-ups). We selected for review some of the recent examinations—conducted by the Office of the Comptroller of the Currency (OCC), Federal Reserve Bank of New York (FRBNY), Federal Deposit Insurance Corporation (FDIC), Securities and Exchange Commission (SEC), and National Futures Association (NFA)—of regulated entities engaged in transactions with hedge funds as creditors or counterparties. We reviewed examinations of financial institutions that are creditors or counterparties to hedge funds conducted from fiscal years 2004 through 2006 and other supervisory materials. We reviewed 3 OCC examinations, 7 FRBNY examinations, 1 FDIC examination, 14 (9 for hedge fund advisers and 5 for Consolidated Supervised Entities) SEC examinations, and 4 NFA examinations. We reviewed information that the federal financial regulators provided on enforcement cases brought for hedge fund-related activities. In addition, we interviewed U.S. federal financial regulatory officials to gain an understanding of how they oversee hedge fund-related activities at the financial institutions over which they have regulatory authority. More specifically, we spoke with officials from the banking regulators—OCC, Board of Governors of the Federal Reserve System, FRBNY, FDIC, and Office of Thrift Supervision; a securities regulator— SEC; and commodities regulators—Commodity Futures Trading Commission and NFA. We interviewed officials representing Department of Treasury (Treasury), the United Kingdom's Financial Services Authority, and the President's Working Group (PWG) as well. To determine which of the Institutional Investor's *Alpha Magazine* 2007 Annual Hedge Fund 100 listing of global hedge fund advisers were U.S.- based and registered with SEC as a hedge fund investment adviser or with CFTC as a commodity pool operator (CPO) or commodity trading advisor (CTA), we asked the compliance staff at SEC and NFA to compare their registrants' listing with the largest 100 listing. Representatives from both organizations said that they made their best attempt to match the names in the largest 100 listing with the registrants' listings, which was difficult because the names were not always identical in both listings. SEC estimates that of the 78 of the largest 100 hedge fund advisers identified by *Alpha Magazine* as U.S.-based, 49 were registered with SEC as investment advisers. NFA estimates that 29 of the 78 U.S.- based hedge fund advisers were registered with CFTC as CPOs or CTAs. We also reviewed prior GAO reports.[55]

To address the second objective (market discipline), we interviewed relevant market participants (such as investors, creditors, and counterparties), and regulatory officials, to get their opinions on (1) how market participants impose market discipline on hedge funds' risk taking and leveraging (and whether they have improved since 1998); (2) the type and frequency of information such participants would need from hedge fund advisers to gauge funds' risk profiles and internal controls to make informed initial and ongoing investment decisions; and (3) the extent to which hedge fund disclosures to market participants have improved since the 1998 near failure of the large hedge fund, Long-Term Capital Management. We also interviewed large hedge funds and the Managed Funds Association—a membership organization representing the hedge fund industry. In addition, we conducted a literature search to identify research on hedge funds and reviewed a selection of relevant regulatory and industry studies, speeches, and testimonies on the matter.

To address the third objective (systemic risk), we reviewed relevant speeches, testimonies, studies, principles and guidelines that the PWG issued about private pools of capital in 2007 entitled "Agreement Among PWG and U.S. Agency Principals on Principles and Guidelines Regarding Private Pools of Capital," regulatory examination documents and relevant industry best practices for investors, hedge fund advisers, creditors, and counterparties. We also reviewed PWG protocols ("PWG Crisis Management Protocols") for dealing with a financial market crisis. And we interviewed officials representing U.S. federal financial regulators, Treasury, and the PWG to get their views on systemic risk issues.

To address pension plan investments in hedge funds discussed in appendix II, we reviewed and analyzed annual survey data from 2001 through 2006 from *Pensions & Investments*. Also, we reviewed Greenwich Associates data from 2004 through 2006 that focused on pensions' hedge fund investments.[56] We conducted data reliability assessments on the data from *Pensions & Investments* and Greenwich Associates that we used, and determined that the data were sufficiently reliable for our purposes. We also reviewed provisions of the Pension Protection Act of 2006 (PPA) that changed requirements for how hedge funds hold pension plan assets. We interviewed pension industry officials (such as pension plan sponsors of public and private funds, trade groups, pension consultants, pension plan and hedge fund database providers, a hedge fund law firm, and hedge funds), an academic and regulatory officials from the Department of Labor, SEC, and Treasury to get their opinions on the matter, including trends in such investments over the last few years and the impact of PPA on pension plan hedge fund investments. We also reviewed other relevant documents.

We conducted this performance audit from September 2006 to January 2008 in accordance with generally accepted government auditing standards. Those standards require that we plan and perform the audit to obtain sufficient, appropriate evidence to provide a reasonable basis for our findings and conclusions based on our audit objectives. We believe that the evidence obtained provides a reasonable basis for our findings and conclusions based on our audit objectives.

In: Hedge Funds: Regulation and Nonregulation ISBN: 978-1-60692-041-1
Editor: Yeram E. Torrey, pp. 47-51 © 2009 Nova Science Publishers, Inc.

Appendix II: Pension Plan Investments in Hedge Funds Have Increased but Are Still a Small Percentage of Plans' Total Assets

This appendix presents summary information about the potential impact that pension law reform may have on the ability of hedge funds to attract pension plan investments and statistics on the extent of pension plan investments in hedge funds in recent years.[57]

Section 611(f) of the Pension Protection Act of 2006 (PPA) amended the Employee Retirement Income Security Act (ERISA) to, among other things, provide a statutory definition for "plan assets," which essentially codified, with some modification, the Department of Labor's (DOL)—the primary regulator of pension plans—existing plan asset regulation (sometimes referred to as the 25 percent benefit plan investor test).[58] By modifying the 25 percent benefit plan investor test, the PPA amendment has the effect of permitting hedge funds to accept unlimited investments from certain "non-ERISA benefit plans" (governmental plans, foreign plans, and most church plans) while still accepting investments from plans that are subject to ERISA (ERISA benefit plans) without becoming subject to ERISA's fiduciary duty requirements. What constitutes "plan assets" is significant because a person who exercises discretionary authority or control over the assets of an ERISA benefit plan or who provides investment advice for a fee with respect to plan assets is a "fiduciary" subject to the fiduciary responsibility provisions of ERISA.[59]

As ERISA did not provide a definition for "plan assets" prior to the enactment of PPA, DOL, in 1986, adopted Rule 2510.3-101 to describe the circumstances under which the assets of an entity in which an ERISA benefit plan invests (for example, a hedge fund) would be deemed to include "plan assets" so that the manager of the entity (for example, a hedge fund manager) would be subject to the fiduciary responsibility rules of ERISA.[60] Rule 2510.3-101 excludes from the definition of plan assets, the assets of an entity in which there is no significant aggregate investment by "benefit plan investors," which is defined to include both ERISA and nonERISA benefit plans. Participation in an entity would be significant if 25 percent or more of the value of any class of equity securities of the entity were held by the benefit plan investors collectively (i.e., the 25 percent benefit plan investor rule). By now excluding from the 25 percent calculation those equity securities held by non-ERISA benefit plans, the allowable proportionate share of investments by ERISA benefit plans has increased.

We asked several large hedge funds as well as some regulators whether hedge fund advisers were actively soliciting investments from pension plans due to the reform. They were unable to comment on whether hedge fund advisers were taking steps to attract these institutional investments. However, according to one regulator and two large hedge funds, some hedge fund advisers do not seek pension investments, and others do seek out pension investments but are careful not to reach the 25 percent threshold that would require hedge fund advisers to assume fiduciary responsibilities. According to one regulator and an industry source, pension plans are attracted to various hedge fund investment strategies, depending on their portfolio composition. They also suggested that pension plans tend to invest in hedge funds through funds of hedge funds.

From 2001 through 2006, investments by defined benefit (DB) plans in hedge funds increased, but the share of total pension plan assets invested in hedge funds remained small.[61] Two key reasons pension plans invest in hedge funds are to diversify their investment risks and increase investment returns. Much of the recent growth (and expected continued growth) in hedge fund investments is attributable to investments by institutions such as pension funds, endowments, insurance companies, and foundations.

Two recent surveys of DB plan sponsors describe the prevalence of hedge fund investments.[62]

- According to a Greenwich Associates survey of pensions plans with $250 million or more in assets, the share of private and public DB plans (not including union plans) invested in hedge funds was 27 percent and 24 percent, respectively, in 2006.[63] Among DB plans with $250 million to $500 million in assets, 16 percent were invested in hedge funds. About 29 percent of DB plans with $1 billion or more in assets were invested in hedge funds.

- The number of DB plans investing in hedge funds has increased over time. According to a survey of the largest pension plans by *Pensions & Investments*, the share of DB plans reporting investments in hedge funds increased from 11 percent in 2001 to 36 percent in 2006.[64]

  Evidence from surveys of DB plans shows that between about 1 to 2 percent of total assets were invested in hedge funds.[65] Among only those plans that invested in hedge funds, average allocations to hedge funds ranged from about 3 percent to 7 percent of a plan's portfolio.
- A very small number of pension plans reported substantially larger allocations to hedge funds. Two of the 48 largest pension plans that reported investments in hedge funds in the *Pensions & Investments* survey had allocations of about 30 percent (Missouri State Employees' Retirement System and Pennsylvania State Employees' Retirement System—both of these plans primarily invest in hedge funds through funds of funds). See table 1.
- Survey data indicate that most pension plans invested in hedge funds do so, at least partially, through funds of hedge funds. According to the *Pensions & Investments'* survey, 35 of the largest 48 DB plans that reported investments in hedge funds used funds of hedge funds for at least some of their hedge fund investments. Overall, funds of hedge funds represented 54 percent of total hedge fund investments for this group.

Compared with pension plans, endowments and foundations were much more likely to invest in hedge funds. Greenwich Associates' survey found that 75 percent of endowments and foundations (with at least $250 million in assets) were invested in hedge funds in 2006. These investments amounted to slightly more than 12 percent of total assets for all endowments and foundations in their sample.

According to *Pensions & Investments*, hedge fund investments reported among the largest pension plans increased from about $3.2 billion in 2001 to about $50.5 billion in 2006, approximately a 1,500 percent increase (see fig. 1).

Furthermore, for those DB plans that reported hedge fund investments in the 2006 *Pensions & Investments* survey, the investments represented about 3 percent of their total DB assets under management.

Table 1. Ten Defined Benefit Plans with the Largest Reported Hedge Fund Investments for 2006

(Assets in millions of dollars based on September 2006 data)					
Defined benefit plan	Direct investment	Funds of hedge funds (indirect investment)	Total hedge fund investment	Total DB assets	Total hedge fund investment as a percentage of total DB assets
Pennsylvania State Employees' Retirement System	$1,384	$7,814	$9,198	$30,372	30.3
New York State Common Retirement Fund	655	3,095	3,750	144,289	2.6
California Public Emplo yees' Retirement System	3,710		3,710	217,648	1.7
Massachusetts Pension Reserves Investment Management Board		3,032	3,032	43,535	7.0
General Electric Co.	2,344		2,344	51,736	4.5
Virginia Retirement System	2,209		2,209	50,311	4.4
Missouri State Employees' Retirement System	752	1,443	2,195	7,150	30.7
Pennsylvania Public School Employees' Retirement System	2,098		2,098	58,490	3.6
General Motors Corp.		1,975	1,975	98,612	2.0
Citigroup	1,887		1,887	11,549	16.3
Total	$15,039	$17,359	$32,398	$713,692	4.5%

Source: *Pensions & Investments* (January 2007 annual survey).

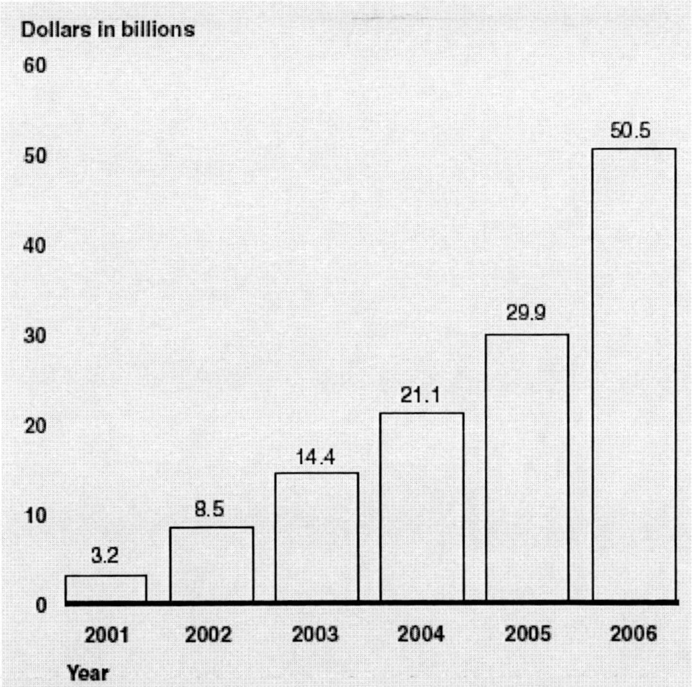

Source: Pensions & Investments.

Note: The investments are aggregated among DB plans in the top 200 pension plans (measured by combined DB and defined contribution assets) surveyed by Pensions & Investments. In 2006, 48 DB plans reported investments in hedge funds.

Figure 1. Investments in Hedge Funds Reported by Defined Benefit Plans for the Period 2001-2006.

In: Hedge Funds: Regulation and Nonregulation ISBN: 978-1-60692-041-1
Editor: Yeram E. Torrey, pp. 53 © 2009 Nova Science Publishers, Inc.

APPENDIX III: VARIOUS HEDGE FUND INVESTMENT STRATEGIES DEFINED

Hedge funds seek absolute rather than relative return—that is, look to make a positive return whether the overall (stock or bond) market is up or down—in a variety of market environments and use various investment styles and strategies, and invest in a wide variety of financial instruments, some of which follow:

Convertible arbitrage: Typically attempt to extract value by purchasing convertible securities while hedging the equity, credit, and interest rate exposures with short positions of the equity of the issuing firm and other appropriate fixed-income related derivatives.

Dedicated shorts: Specialize in short-selling securities that are perceived to be overpriced—typically equities.

Emerging market: Specialize in trading the securities of developing economies.

Equity market neutral: Typically trade long-short portfolios of equities with little directional exposure to the stock market.

Event driven: Specialize in trading corporate events, such as merger transactions or corporate restructuring.

Fixed income arbitrage: Typically trade long-short portfolios of bonds.

Macro: Take bets on directional movements in stocks, bonds, foreign exchange rates, and commodity prices.

Long/short equity: Typically exposed to a long-short portfolio of equities with a long bias.

Managed futures: Specialize in futures trading—typically employing trend following strategies.

In: Hedge Funds: Regulation and Nonregulation ISBN: 978-1-60692-041-1
Editor: Yeram E. Torrey, pp. 55-64 © 2009 Nova Science Publishers, Inc.

REFERENCES

[1] Although there is no statutory definition of hedge funds, the term is commonly used to describe pooled investment vehicles that are privately organized and administered by professional managers and that often engage in active trading of various types of securities and commodity futures and options contracts.

[2] By comparison, assets under management in the mutual fund industry grew from about $5.5 trillion in 1998 to about $10.4 trillion in 2006.

[3] Greenwich Associates, "In U.S. Fixed Income, Hedge Funds Are The Biggest Game In Town," August 30, 2007.

[4] Price discovery refers to the process by which market prices incorporate new information.

[5] A counterparty is the opposite party in a bilateral agreement, contract, or transaction.

[6] The PWG was established by Executive Order 12631, signed on March 18, 1988. The Secretary of the Treasury chairs the PWG, the other members of which are the chairpersons of the Board of Governors of the Federal Reserve System, Securities and Exchange Commission, and Commodity Futures Trading Commission. The group was formed in 1988 to enhance the integrity, efficiency, orderliness, and competitiveness of the U.S. financial markets and maintain the public's confidence in those markets. Prime brokerage is the name for a bundled package of services (e.g., clearance and settlement of securities trades, margin loans, and risk management services) offered by investment banks to hedge funds.

[7] See the President's Working Group on Financial Markets, *Hedge Funds, Leverage, and the Lessons of Long-Term Capital Management* (April 28, 1999).

[8] For example, in fall 2006, a fund operated by Amaranth Advisors, LLC, lost more than $6 billion as a result of natural gas trading. In summer 2007, two hedge funds sponsored by Bear Stearns Asset Management experienced losses from its holdings of collateralized debt obligations (CDO) that contained subprime mortgages. A CDO is a security backed by a pool of bonds, loans, or other assets.

[9] Federal Reserve Chairman Ben S. Bernanke, *The Recent Financial Turmoil and Its Economic and Policy Consequence* (Speech at the Economic Club of New York, Oct. 15, 2007).

[10] Systemic risk generally is defined as the risk that a disruption (at a firm, in a market segment, to a settlement system, etc.) could be transmitted to and potentially pose risks to other firms, other market segments, or the financial system as a whole.

[11] NFA is a self-regulatory organization for the U.S. futures industry.

[12] We do not discuss OTS's examination program in this report because at the time of our review OTS officials noted that no thrifts were making loans to hedge funds or serving in any significant trading counterparty capacity.

[13] The hedge funds themselves are not registered with any regulators.

[14] We were not able to find any estimate of the total number of hedge fund advisers.

[15] Except as may otherwise be provided by law, a CPO is an individual or organization that operates an enterprise, and who, in connection therewith, solicits or receives funds from third parties, for the purpose of trading in any commodity for future delivery on a contract market or derivatives execution facility. 7 U.S.C. § 1a(5). A CTA is, except as otherwise provided by law, any person who, for compensation or profit, (1) directly or indirectly advises others on the advisability of buying or selling any contract of sale of a commodity for future delivery, commodity options or certain leverage transactions contracts, or (2) as part of a regular business, issues analyses or reports concerning the activities in clause (1). 7 U.S.C. § 1a(6). In addition to statutory exclusions to the definition of CPO and CTA, CFTC has promulgated regulations setting forth additional criteria under which a person may be excluded from the definition of CPO or CTA. See 17 C.F.R. §§ 4.5 and 4.6 7(2007).

[16] A horizontal review is a coordinated supervisory review of a specific activity, business line, or risk management practice conducted across a group of peer institutions.

[17] Stress testing measures the potential impact of various scenarios or market movements on an asset, counterparty exposure, or the value of a firm's portfolio.

[18] Counterparty credit risk is the risk that a loss will be incurred if a counterparty to a transaction does not fulfill its financial obligations in a timely manner.

[19] To avoid being required to register as an investment company under the Investment Company Act of 1940 (Investment Company Act), hedge funds typically rely on sections 3(c)(1) or 3(c)(7) of that act. Section 3(c)(1) excludes from the definition of "investment company" under the Investment Company Act hedge funds that do not make or propose to make a public offering of their shares and whose share are not beneficially owned by more than 100 investors. 15 U.S.C. § 80a-3(c)(1). Section 3(c)(7) excludes from the definition of "investment company" hedge funds that do not make or propose to make a public offering of their shares and whose shares are offered exclusively by "qualified purchasers" and is exempt from most of the provisions of the Investment Company Act. 15 U.S.C. § 80a- 3(c)(7). Generally, "qualified purchasers" are individuals who own at least $5 million in investments or companies that own at least $25 million in investments. 15 U.S.C. § 80a- 2(a)(51). Hedge fund advisers also typically satisfy the "private manager" exemption from registration under section 203(b)(3) of the Investments Advisers Act of 1940 (Advisers Act). Section 203(b)(3) exempts from registration an adviser (1) that has had fewer than 15 clients in the 12 months preceding the claim of exemption and (2) that neither holds himself out generally to the public as an investment adviser nor acts as an investment adviser to any registered investment company or any "business development company" as defined under the Investment Company Act. 15 U.S.C. § 80b-3. Unless its falls within an exclusion from the definition of CPA or CTA, a hedge fund or hedge fund adviser that trades on U.S. commodity futures or option markets, may be subject to the registration requirement under the Commodity Exchange Act (CEA) for CPOs or CTAs, respectively. CFTC has promulgated regulations setting forth criteria for exemption from registration under the CEA. See 17 C.F.R. §§ 4.13 and 4.14 (2007). However, a person claiming to fall outside of the definition of CPO or CTA, as well as those CPOs and CTAs claiming an exemption from registration must file with the NFA a notice of eligibility for the claimed exclusion or exemption, as the case may be, and must submit to any special calls the CFTC may make to require the person to demonstrate its eligibility for such exclusion or exemption.

[20] Under the Securities Act of 1933, a public offering or sale of securities must be registered with SEC, unless otherwise exempted. In order to exempt an offering or sale of hedge fund shares (ownership interests) to investors from registration under the Securities Act of 1933, most hedge funds restrict their sales to accredited investors in compliance with the safe harbor requirements of Rule 506 of Regulation D. See 15 U.S.C. § 77d and § 77e; 17 C.F.R. § 230.506 (2007). Such investors must meet certain wealth and income thresholds. SEC generally has proposed a rule that would raise the accredited investor qualification standards for individual investors (natural persons) from $1 million in net worth to $2.5 million in investments. See *Revisions to Limited Offering Exemptions in Regulation D*, 72 Fed. Reg. 45116 (Aug. 10, 2007) (proposed rules and request for additional comments). In addition, hedge funds typically limit the number of investors to fewer than 500, so as not to fall within the purview of Section 12(g) of the Securities Exchange Act of 1934, which requires the registration of any class of equity securities (other than exempted securities) held of record by 500 or more persons. 15 U.S.C. § 78l(g).

[21] Leverage is the use of various financial instruments or borrowed capital to increase the potential return of an investment. Short selling is the selling of a security that the seller does not own, or any sale that is completed by the delivery of a security borrowed by the seller.

[22] See 15 U.S.C. § 78m(d), (g) and 17 C.F.R. §§ 240.13d-1 *et seq*. (2007).

[23] See 15 U.S.C. § 78m(f) and 17 C.F.R. 240.13f-1 (2007). For purposes of this provision "institutional investment manager" is defined as "any person, other than a natural person, investing in or buying and selling securities for its own account, and any person exercising investment discretion with respect to the account of any person."

[24] See *Registration under the Advisers Act of Certain Hedge Fund Advisers*, 69 Fed. Reg. 72087 (Dec. 10, 2004). The rule essentially amended the definition of "client" so that rather than viewing a hedge fund as a single client of the hedge fund advisers, all limited partners investing in the hedge fund were deemed to be a client, thereby putting the number of clients well above the 14-client limit for the private adviser exemption. The new rule did not require the registration of advisers to funds with certain characteristics, such as a lockup periods of 2 years or more—typically venture capital and private equity funds.

[25] See *Goldstein v. Securities and Exchange Commission*, 451 F.3d 873 (D.C. Cir. 2006). In *Goldstein*, the U.S. Circuit Court of Appeals for the District of Columbia held that SEC's hedge fund rule was arbitrary because it

departed, without reasonable justification, from SEC's long-standing interpretation of the term "client" in the private adviser exemption as referring to the hedge fund itself, and not to the individual investors in the fund. See footnote 19, *supra*, for a description of the private adviser exemption from registration under the Advisers Act.

[26] According to the May 2007 edition of Institutional Investor's *Alpha Magazine*, which lists the largest 100 global hedge funds based on assets as of December 31, 2006, 78 of the largest 100 hedge funds are U.S.-based hedge funds. According to HedgeFund Intelligence, $1.5 trillion in hedge fund assets were under management in the United States as of March 2007.

[27] See GAO, *Securities and Exchange Commission: Steps Being Taken to Make Examination Program More Risk-Based and Transparent*, GAO-07-1053 (Washington, D.C.: Aug. 14, 2007).

[28] SEC did not identify the largest U.S. hedge funds cited in industry reports prior to conducting these hedge fund adviser examinations. Twenty-seven of the largest hedge fund advisers were examined by SEC from fiscal years 2005 to 2007.

[29] For non-hedge fund investment advisers, the percentage that received a deficiency letter is 84 percent.

[30] See *Supervised Investment Bank Holding Companies*, 69 Fed. Reg. 34472 (Jun. 21, 2004) [codified primarily at 17 C.F.R. § 240.17i-1 *et seq.*]. Section 17(i) of the Securities Exchange Act authorizes SEC to supervise investment bank holding companies (IBHCs) on a consolidated basis. An IBHC is any person (other than a natural person) that owns or controls one or more brokers or dealers, and the associated persons of the IBHC. 15 U.S.C. § 78q(i)(5)(A). The CSE program implements section § 17(i). The purpose of the CSE program is to reduce the likelihood that weaknesses in the holding company or an unregulated affiliate (such as a CSE-owned hedge fund) endangers a regulated entity or the broader financial system, to provide consolidated oversight for internationally active firms required to meet international consolidated supervisor requirements established by the European Union's Financial Conglomerates Directive, and to meet a PWG recommendation to expand risk assessment authority for the unregulated affiliates of broker-dealers.

[31] The five CSEs are: Merrill Lynch & Co., Inc.; Morgan Stanley Inc.; Bear Stearns Companies Inc.; Goldman Sachs Group, Inc.; and Lehman Brothers Holdings Inc.

[32] SEC is required by statute: (1) to focus its CSE examinations to the holding company, its associated registered broker-dealers and any affiliates that

could have a material adverse effect on the operational or financial condition of the broker or dealer; and (2) with respect to affiliates of the holding company that are banks, licensed insurance companies and certain other financial institutions, to defer to the appropriate federal banking agencies and state insurance regulators with regard to all interpretations of, and the enforcement of applicable federal banking laws and state insurance laws relating to the activities and operations of such affiliates. 15 U.S.C. § 78a(i)(3)-(4).

[33] Basel regulatory capital standards were developed by the Basel Committee on Banking Supervision, which consists of central bank and regulatory officials from 13 member countries. The standards aim to align minimum capital requirements with enhanced risk measurement techniques and to encourage internationally actively banks to develop a more disciplined approach to risk management.

[34] A cross-firm review is a coordinated supervisory review of a specific activity, business line, or risk management practice conducted across a group of peer institutions. All five of the CSEs were reviewed.

[35] According to CFTC officials, the LTRS captures 70 to 90 percent of the daily activity on registered futures exchanges.

[36] FCMs are individuals, associations, partnerships, corporations, or trusts that solicit or accept orders for the purchase or sale of any commodity for future delivery on or subject to the rules of any contract market or derivatives transaction execution facility; and in connection with such solicitation or acceptance of orders, accept money, securities, or property (or extend credit in lieu thereof) to margin, guarantee, or secure any trades or contracts that result or may result therefrom.

[37] In the CFTC complaint filed against Amaranth Advisors, LLC; Amaranth Advisors (Calgary), ULC, and Brian Hunter, CFTC alleged that the defendants attempted to manipulate the price of natural gas contracts on the New York Mercantile Exchange, Inc., in 2006. Complaint for Injunctive and Other Equitable Relief and Civil Monetary Penalties under the Commodity Exchange Act, *CFTC v. Amaranth Advisors, LLC*, No. 07-6682 (S.D.N.Y., July 25, 2007).

[38] Because "hedge fund" is not a defined term under the CEA or any other federal statute, CFTC and NFA records do not identify whether a commodity pool is a hedge fund. Thus, CFTC cannot report on the exact number of examinations that involve hedge funds. In the event the CPO or CTA self-designates itself as a hedge fund, the Division of Enforcement typically incorporates that designation in the enforcement action, and that

designation is often used in the press release notifying the public of the enforcement action.

[39] A registered CPO or CTA seeking to engage in futures business with the public or with any member of NFA must itself be a member of NFA.

[40] For the purpose of this report the term "hedge fund advisers" includes, as the context requires, CPOs, CTAs, or securities investment advisers.

[41] Testimony of Kevin Warsh, Governor, Board of Governors of the Federal Reserve Board System, before the House Committee on Financial Services, 110th Congress, 1st Sess., July 11, 2007.

[42] Liquidity risk is the potential that a firm will be unable to meet its obligations as they come due because of an inability to liquidate assets or obtain adequate funding or that it cannot easily unwind or offset specific exposures without significantly lowering market prices because of inadequate market depth or market disruptions.

[43] According to an SEC report and some market participants we interviewed, PPMs discuss in broad terms the fund's investment strategies and practices; risk factors; information on the general partner or investment manager; management fees and incentive compensation; key personnel of the fund manager; synopsis of the limited partnership agreement or other organizational documents; conflicts of interest; side letters (preferential redemption terms that may be granted to one class of investors) and side pockets (illiquid investments held separately from the primary fund); investment, withdrawal, and transfer procedures; and valuation.

[44] ERISA § 404(a)(1)(B) [29 U.S.C. 1104(a)(1)(B)] requires a fiduciary to act with the care, skill, prudence, and diligence under the prevailing circumstances that a prudent person acting in a like capacity and familiar with such matters would use.

[45] MFA is a hedge fund trade group. CRMPG is an industry policy group that formed in 1999 after the near collapse of LTCM and comprises the 12 largest internationally active commercial and investment banks. IOSCO is an international organization that brings together the regulators of the world's securities and futures markets. IOSCO and its sister organizations, the Basel Committee on Banking Supervision and the International Association of Insurance Supervisors, make up the Joint Forum of international financial regulators.

[46] Value at risk is a calculation used to determine the amount that could be expected to be lost from an investment or a portfolio of investments over a specified time under certain circumstances.

[47] A derivative is a financial instrument, such as an option or futures contract, the value of which depends on the performance of an underlying security or asset. Securities financing transactions include repurchase agreements, securities lending transactions, and other types of borrowing transactions that, in economic substance, utilize securities as collateral for the extension of credit. A repurchase agreement is a financial transaction in which a dealer borrows money by selling securities and simultaneously agreeing to buy them back at a later date.

[48] According to the literature, (1) current exposure represents the current replacement cost of financial instrument transactions, i.e., their current market value; (2) potential exposure is an estimate of the future replacement cost of financial instrument transactions; and (3) an initial margin is the good-faith deposit that protects the counterparty against a loss from adverse market movements in the interval between periodic marking-to-market.

[49] See Counterparty Risk Management Policy Group II, *Toward Greater Financial Stability: A Private Sector Perspective* (July 27, 2005).

[50] Reasons cited by CRMPG for a reduction in the probability of systemic financial shock from hedge fund activity included (1) the strength of the key financial institutions at the core of the financial system, (2) improved risk management techniques, (3) improved official supervision, (4) more effective disclosure and greater transparency, (5) strengthened financial infrastructure, and (6) more effective techniques to hedge and widely distribute financial risk.

[51] Testimony of Randal K. Quarles, Under Secretary for Domestic Finance, Department of the Treasury, before the Senate Committee on Banking, Housing, and Urban Affairs, 110th Congress, 1st Sess., July 25, 2006.

[52] Roger T. Cole, Greg Feldberg, and David Lynch, "Hedge Funds, Credit Risk Transfer and Financial Stability," *Financial Stability Review*, April 2007, p. 13.

[53] Cole, Feldberg, and Lynch, "Hedge Funds, Credit Risk Transfer and Financial Stability," p. 15.

[54] For example, according to press reports, the tightening of credit markets that followed the collapse of two Bear Stearns-sponsored hedge funds in June 2007 was partly triggered by a revaluation of the CDOs. Merrill Lynch, one of the funds' prime brokers, seized $850 million of the funds assets held as collateral, including CDOs, but it reportedly only sold a fraction of the assets because the value of these securities had fallen.

[55] See GAO, *Commodity Futures Trading Commission: Trends in Energy Derivatives Markets Raise Questions about CFTC's Oversight*, GAO-08-25

(Washington, D.C.: Oct. 19, 2007); *Credit Derivatives: Confirmation Backlogs Increased Dealers' Operational Risks, but Were Successfully Addressed after Joint Regulatory Action*, GAO-07-716 (Washington, D.C.: June 13, 2007); *Financial Market Regulation: Agencies Engaged in Consolidated Supervision Can Strengthen Performance Measurement and Collaboration*, GAO-07-154 (Washington, D.C.: Mar. 15, 2007); and *Long-Term Capital Management: Regulators Need to Focus Greater Attention on Systemic Risk*, GAO/GGD-00-3 (Washington, D.C.: Oct. 29, 1999).

[56] *Pensions & Investments* is an industry publication that has conducted the annual survey for the last 33 years. Greenwich and Associates is an institutional financial services consulting and research firm.

[57] A forthcoming GAO report (to be issued in the summer of 2008) will provide more detailed information about various aspects of pension plan investments in hedge funds.

[58] Pub. L. No. 109-280, § 611(f), 120 Stat. 952, 972 (2006) (codified at 29 U.S.C. § 1002(42)).

[59] Section 3(21) of ERISA defines "fiduciary." 29 U.S.C. § 1002(21).

[60] See *Final Regulation Relating to the Definition of Plan Assets*, 51 Fed. Reg. 41262 (Nov. 13, 1986) (final rule codified at 29 C.F.R. 2510.3-101). Rule 2510.3-101 describes what constitutes "plan assets" with respect to a plan's investment in another entity for purposes of Subtitle A (definitional and coverage provisions) and Parts 1 and 4 (reporting and disclosure and fiduciary provisions) of Subtitle B of ERISA and for purposes of section 4975 of the Internal Revenue Code (excise tax provisions relating to prohibited transactions).

[61] Defined benefit plans commonly provide a guaranteed monthly benefit based on a formula that considers salary and years of service to a company. Defined contribution plan benefits are based on contributions and investment returns (gains and losses).

[62] If pension plan sponsors have more than one DB plan, they may collectively manage assets for these plans and thus may provide survey answers for the combined fund, rather than for each individual pension plan.

[63] Greenwich Associates surveyed pension plans, endowments, and foundations, that had a minimum of $250 million in assets and used at least two external investment advisers. Greenwich Associates obtained asset allocation information regarding hedge funds from 584 of the 652 DB plans it interviewed in 2006.

[64] The top 200 pension plans surveyed by *Pensions & Investments* are ranked by combined assets in DB and defined contribution plans. These plans

reported almost $6 billion or more in combined DB and defined contribution assets in 2006. Of these top 200 pension plans, 135 were DB plans that completed the survey and provided asset allocation information, and 48 of these plans reported investments in hedge funds in 2006.

[65] Survey data were not available for DB plans with less than $200 million in assets.

INDEX

D

E

F

G

H

I

J

L

M

S

T